Antje Gillingham

KNITTING
circles around
SOCKS

knit two at a time on circular needles

Martingale®
& C O M P A N Y

CREDITS

President & CEO • Tom Wierzbicki

Publisher • Jane Hamada

Editorial Director • Mary V. Green

Managing Editor • Tina Cook

Developmental Editor • Karen Costello Soltys

Technical Editor • Ursula Reikes

Copy Editor • Liz McGehee

Design Director • Stan Green

Assistant Design Director • Regina Girard

Illustrator • Robin Strobel

Cover & Text Designer • Shelly Garrison

Photographer • Brent Kane

MISSION STATEMENT

Dedicated to providing quality products
and service to inspire creativity.

Knitting Circles around Socks: Knit Two at a Time on Circular Needles
© 2007 by Antje Gillingham

Martingale & Company
20205 144th Ave. NE
Woodinville, WA 98072-8478 USA
www.martingale-pub.com

Printed in China
12 11 10 09 08 07   8 7 6 5 4 3 2

Library of Congress Cataloging-in-Publication Data
Library of Congress Control Number: 2007014237

ISBN: 978-1-56477-739-3

DEDICATION

To Terry, my Love, who quietly did all the household chores while I knitted, who patiently listened to pattern ideas while I typed, and whose support, encouragement, and belief in my abilities never once faltered.

ACKNOWLEDGMENTS

I would like to thank Maryann Brown for knitting her little fingers to the bone while working on many 7" sock feet as I heart-lessly piled up unfinished socks with barely turned heels in front of her, for test knitting pattern after pattern, for catching even the smallest discrepancy, and for giving valuable input on how to clarify and simplify certain instructions; Marilyn Evans for patiently test knitting several patterns; both ladies and all my customers and friends for their boundless encouragement and support. I couldn't have done it without all of you.

Contents

PREFACE • 6

INTRODUCTION • 8

GETTING STARTED • 10

KNITTING BASICS • 13

THE BASIC SOCK PATTERN • 20

CHUNKY, COZY COTTON SOCKS • 34   ANNE'S MAGIC STRIPES • 38

DAZZLING BEADS • 42   CABLED CORN • 48

ANKLETS AND RUFFLES • 54

FIXATION ON STRIPES • 58

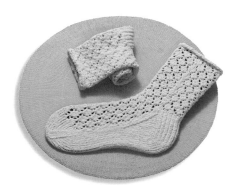

FIXATION ON LACE • 62

DIAMONDS AND LACE • 68

CONVERTING PATTERNS FROM
DOUBLE-POINTED TO CIRCULAR NEEDLES • 75

ABBREVIATIONS AND GLOSSARY • 77

USEFUL INFORMATION • 78

YARN SOURCES • 79

Preface

My husband likes to tell people I learned how to knit back in the "Old World," which I suppose is correct. But does he really have to put *old* and *me* into the same sentence just because I was born a little while back in Germany and learned the ancient art of knitting in fourth grade? At the time, *ancient* meant "Oma's (grandma's) hobby," not the fact that knitting truly is a very old craft.

My choices for yarn were limited—wool, cotton, acrylic—and since I was eight years old, I was handed acrylic. I remember making a huge striped snake. The experience left me scarred for life and with a serious handicap for weaving and seaming.

A few years ago, I went to visit my friend Alice in California, and one afternoon I found myself alone with nothing to do. I drove 20 minutes to Pacific Grove, thinking I would saunter away the afternoon in its quaint little downtown. I was in search of a good parking spot when suddenly, there it was, a little yarn shop almost hidden from sight. A wooden mannequin stood outside its doors dressed in nothing but a huge fluffy sweater.

It was the first yarn shop I had seen in years, and it catapulted me back in time. Instantly, I had visions of my stepmother and me sitting in the living room on a cold winter day drinking tea all cozy and warm, knitting. I remembered our occasional trips to yarn stores in Germany, and suddenly it felt like I'd been missing knitting desperately. I remembered a calming, relaxing sensation, which had enveloped me each time I'd picked up my needles in the past. I was taken aback by this sudden onslaught of feelings and did the only thing I *could* do! I quickly found a parking space and made my way to the yarn shop.

As I climbed up the steps, I caught a glimpse of color through the windowpanes. My heart beat faster, then I pushed through the door and stepped into what I can only describe as a knitter's heaven. My hand fluttered to my mouth and I barely breathed, "oh." I am only glad nobody walked in after me, destroying the wonderful, utterly overwhelming sensation I experienced just looking around.

The shop was small, and containers stuffed full of yarn not only stacked bottom to top against walls but also jutted out into the middle here and there, creating little aisles to explore. I stretched out my hand and thrust it into the closest basket. My fingers closed around a supersoft ball of yarn, I petted it, and after that there was no stopping me.

I wandered through the store, sticking my hands into every single basket and container I came across. I closed my eyes and murmured aahs and oohs. People were staring, but I didn't care. I discovered fluff and ribbon, fur and eyelash, sparkle and glitz, soft and cozy; most importantly though, I rediscovered knitting. Suddenly, I saw endless possibilities, and before I even stepped out of the store with a huge bag full of treasures, I had found passion. That night, back at Alice's house, I cast on the first stitches in a very long time and I was hopelessly and completely hooked.

Back home in Maryville, Tennessee, I immediately bombarded my poor unsuspecting husband with ideas of opening a knitting shop downtown. He was very supportive and less than a year later, the Knitting Nest was born. Today, three years after the grand opening, my cozy little shop has evolved into something I never dreamed of. Much more than a mere retail store where you can buy yarn and knitting supplies, it is a place of social gathering, a sanctuary, where friends meet to share a passion (sometimes obsession) for needlecraft, texture, and color.

My customers always tell me that, to them, knitting is therapy. Together, we have conquered everything from washcloths and scarves to seamless sweaters and summer tops. One of my most popular workshops is Knitting Two Socks on Two Circular Needles. I love the ability of knitting both socks at the same time. They'll always be the same length and when you are done with the pair, you are done! You don't have to put the first sock aside and now do the exact same thing for the second one.

If you know how to knit and purl, then you can knit socks on circular needles. As with any new pattern, the beginning can be confusing and at times disheartening. I've tried to be extremely thorough with my instructions and pictures in this book. My students have been an invaluable help with questions and suggestions on how to clarify certain steps even better. In other words, all patterns have been tried several times. I have also used different weights and kinds of yarn for you to experiment with, but with a little practice, you can transfer any double-pointed-needle sock pattern to two circular needles.

Like my little shop, this book, too, is a sanctuary, and you, dear reader, are a friend who has stopped by to see what's new. Visit a while and knit with me—it's so good to see you.

—Antje

Introduction

Hand-knitted socks are experiencing a huge surge in popularity, and today's multitude of gorgeous self-patterned sock yarn is only partly responsible. Aside from being a small handy project that can be taken anywhere without much ado, there is something very satisfying about knitting a pair of socks.

However, there are two things that will stop knitters dead in their tracks. One is the idea of having to work with pesky double-pointed needles, and the other is the fact that they'll have to knit the exact same thing twice. *Knitting Circles around Socks* introduces a technique that uses two circular needles and a basic pattern, teaching knitters

to work both socks simultaneously. There are numerous patterns included, beginning with an easy basic sock and ending with cables, beads, and lace work. The instructions are supported by many pictures and illustrations to make the learning process less frustrating and more fun. The book also includes simple steps to help convert any sock pattern from double-pointed to circular needles, thus opening the door to limitless sock imagination. It is the stepping-stone to turning sock knitting into *one* exciting, relatively quick project rather than repetitive knitting that consists of constant measuring and stitch-and-row counting to duplicate an already-completed sock.

Getting Started

Here, you'll find information about the parts of socks, sock sizes, and the importance of knitting a gauge.

SOCK TERMINOLOGY

Terminology can be so darn confusing. What is a gusset? Where does the heel end and the sole begin? These illustrations should help clarify the exact location of the different parts and measurements that make up a sock.

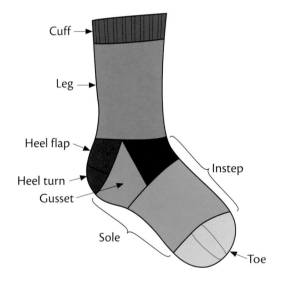

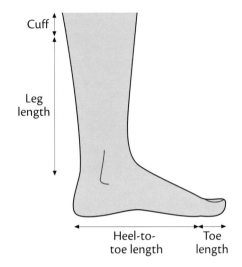

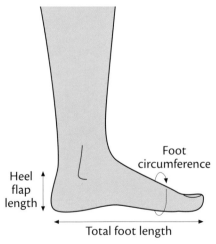

GAUGE

Ah, the gauge. Most of us hate it. I am a very lazy person when it comes to gauging. But a few knitting disasters forced me to knit a gauge before every project. I drill it into my students as well: knit that gauge, I say, if you want your stuff to fit, and sometimes I show them what happens when you don't.

The problem is that we want to start that new project with the gorgeous yarn *now*. But, like flossing, knitting a gauge is necessary, although tedious. It will assure the correct fit and look of your project, especially if you use expensive or substituted yarn or if you work on, say, two socks simultaneously. The alternative of ripping out all your hard work is even more painful; believe me, I've been there many times. So just bite into that sour apple, knit a swatch, and check those pesky little stitches.

Most patterns tell you the stitch count over 4". I tell my students to knit the gauge swatch 6" wide and 6" long. If you try to measure the stitches in a 4" x 4" swatch, they will be distorted and incorrect. Always cast on a few more stitches and knit a little longer to be sure that your gauge is accurate.

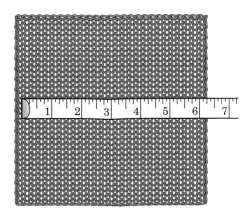

SOCK SIZES

The instructions in this book are for socks for women. However, you can alter the size of any sock to fit a child or man by simply casting on a different number of stitches and working the parts of the sock to the appropriate measurements for a given shoe size. Approximate measurements are provided for children's, women's, and men's sizes.

SHOE SIZE	CUFF CIRCUMFERENCE (IN INCHES)	HEEL-FLAP LENGTH (IN INCHES)	HEEL-TO-TOE LENGTH (IN INCHES)	TOE LENGTH (IN INCHES)
CHILDREN				
3–4	5¼	1	3¼	1
5–6	5½	1¼	3¾	1¼
7–8	5¾	1½	4½	1¼
9–10	6¼	1½	5	1½
11–12	6¾	1¾	6	1½
13	7	1¾	6½	1½
1–2	7¼	1¾	6½	1½
3–4	7½	2	6¾	1½
WOMEN				
5	7¾	2	6¾	1½
6	7¾	2¼	7	1¾
7–8	8	2¼	7	1¾
9	8¼	2¼	7¼	2
10	8¼	2½	7½	2
11	8½	2½	7¾	2
MEN				
8–9	8¼	2¼	7¾	2
10	8½	2½	8	2¼
11	8½	2½	8¼	2¼
12	8½	2¾	8½	2½
13	8¾	2¾	8½	2½
14	8¾	2¾	8¾	2½
15	9	2¾	8¾	2½

Knitting Basics

The following techniques are used to make the patterns in this book.

LONG-TAIL CAST ON

There are many different ways to cast on, and they are *all* right ways. I've used the long-tail cast-on method throughout the patterns in this book because its elasticity is great for the cuffs of socks. Of course, you can use any other method to cast on your socks. Most importantly, don't force yourself to learn this cast on just to use with these patterns. Use the one you are familiar with; it's less confusing and will work just fine.

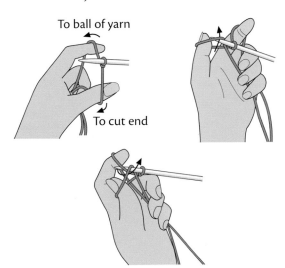

To ball of yarn

To cut end

1. Pull the tail end from the ball of yarn and let a sufficient amount hang down to accommodate the stitches to be cast on. Make a slipknot and slide it onto one of the needles. The tail end should face you. Hold the needle in your right hand.

   Squeeze your left thumb and index finger together and spread the remaining three fingers straight out. Slip the thumb and index finger (still squeezed together) between the two strands of yarn so that the tail hangs over the thumb, and the working yarn hangs over the index finger. Grab the two strands of yarn, which are lying across your palm, with the remaining three fingers, and open the thumb and index finger to look like an imaginary gun. Make sure the inside of the left hand faces you, and the needle tip points to the thumb.

2. Move the needle toward you and all the way down until it reaches the base of the thumb. Slide the needle under the outside strand of yarn wrapped around the thumb and up through the loop in front of the thumb.

3. Now move the needle over and behind the strand of yarn wrapped around the index finger and scoop it up. Next, guide the needle from the top back into the loop in front of the thumb, down and toward you. Let the thumb slip from

under the yarn strand and gently pull the front strand down to tighten the stitch on the needle. Remember, you don't want the stitches too tight around the needle. Instead, they should be slightly bigger with space left for you to start knitting the first round.

Repeat steps 2 and 3 until the required amount of stitches have been cast on.

DECREASES

As with the cast on, there are many different ways to work decreases in a project to make it look nice and neat. Here, the stitches are forced to *slant* a certain way to accommodate the necessary shaping of a garment. In the case of socks, for example, the correct toe shaping is crucial for both fit and appearance as it has to be decreased on both sides to accommodate the shape of the toes. The stitches have to slant inward, meaning on the right side to the left and on the left side to the right.

KNIT TWO TOGETHER (K2TOG) (RIGHT SLANT)

Instead of knitting the next stitch (K1), pass the needle through the next two stitches knitwise and knit them off your needle as if they were one stitch. You've decreased one stitch.

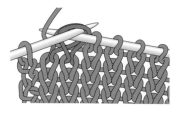

PURL TWO TOGETHER (P2TOG) (RIGHT SLANT)

Here, you purl two stitches together. You've decreased one stitch.

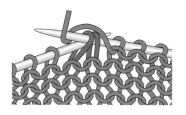

SLIP, SLIP, KNIT (SSK) (LEFT SLANT)

1. Slip one stitch as if to knit, then slip the next stitch as if to knit. I know it sounds redundant, but each stitch has to be slipped individually to get the correct effect.

2. After both stitches have been slipped and are sitting on the right-hand needle, take the left-hand needle and slide it through the front of both stitches, but don't slip them back.

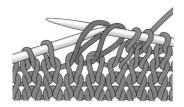

3. The right-hand needle is now sitting behind the left-hand needle. Use the right-hand needle to knit the two stitches together through the back loops of the stitches. It will seem a little awkward but it's pretty easy to get used to. You've decreased one stitch.

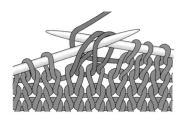

SLIP, SLIP, PURL (SSP) (LEFT SLANT)

Slip, slip, purl is worked on the wrong side of your project, but it creates a left slant on the right side. This step is a bit tricky; let's take it nice and slow. The right-hand needle tip faces away from the left-hand needle tip when you begin. To purl two stitches together through the back, both needle tips have to face in the same direction: to the right.

1. Slip one stitch as if to knit, then slip the next stitch as if to knit. Now move both stitches back to the left-hand needle.

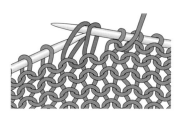

2. Insert the right-hand needle through the back loops of the slipped stitches from left to right, then toward you to the front and left again. Now you are able to purl the two stitches off the left-hand needle. You've decreased one stitch.

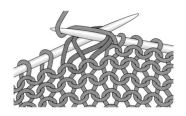

SLIP ONE, KNIT ONE, PASS SLIPPED STITCH OVER (SKP) (LEFT SLANT)

Slip one stitch as if to purl, knit one stitch, pass the slipped stitch over the knit stitch and off the right-hand needle. You've decreased one stitch.

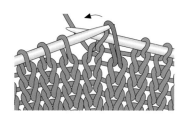

DOUBLE CENTRAL DECREASE (SK2P)

1. Slip one stitch as if to knit, knit the next two stitches together. Both the slipped stitch and the new knit stitch sit on the right-hand needle.

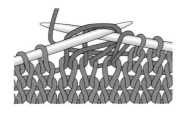

2. Pass the slipped stitch over the knit stitch and off the right-hand needle. You've decreased two stitches.

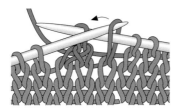

SLIP TWO, KNIT ONE, PASS TWO SLIPPED STITCHES OVER (SL 2, K1, P2SSO)

1. Slip two stitches together as if to knit, knit one stitch.

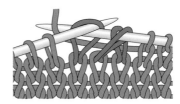

2. Pass the two slipped stitches over the knit stitch and off the right-hand needle. You've decreased two stitches.

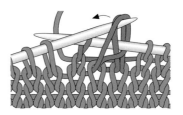

MAKE ONE STITCH (M1)

I used this increase for the socks in this book.
Slip the left-hand needle under the horizontal bar
located between two stitches, from back to front.
Notice how this "new" stitch is twisted. With the
right-hand needle, knit into the front as with any
other stitch. You've increased one stitch.

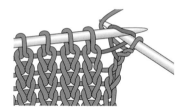

Insert left needle from back to
front under horizontal bar.

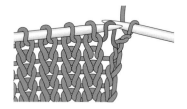

Knit into front of stitch.

SINGLE CROCHET

A row of single crochet cleans up any unruly
edge quite nicely and is easy to do, even for a
noncrocheter like me!

1. Make a slipknot, slip the crochet hook through
    the stitch from front to back right below the
    edge of the sock, slide the slipknot onto the
    hook, and pull it through the stitch to the front.
    You have one stitch on your crochet hook; this is
    your anchor stitch. Chain 1.

2. Insert the hook through the next stitch, yarn over
    the hook, and pull the yarn through the stitch
    from back to front. You'll have two loops on
    your hook.

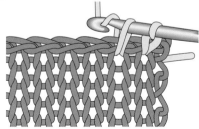

3. Yarn over the hook and pull the yarn through
    both loops on the hook, leaving you with one
    loop again.

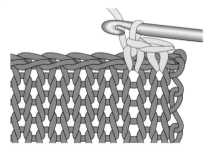

Repeat steps 2 and 3 as needed; cut yarn and
pull through last loop.

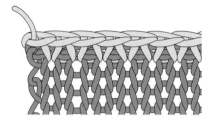

Finished bound-off edge

THE KITCHENER STITCH BIND OFF (GRAFTING)

Everybody is scared of the kitchener stitch, this strange weaving technique that's nothing short of utterly confusing. But even though we don't quite understand it, its effect on a sock toe is simply amazing.

Hold the sock in your left hand, right side facing outward. The yarn tail hangs on the right side of the work and one needle sits in front of the other. Thread the yarn onto the tapestry needle. As you weave the yarn through the stitches, make sure you pass it under the needles back and forth at all times.

When starting the kitchener stitch in the normal manner (work the first stitch on the front needle purlwise and work the first stitch on the back needle knitwise), I noticed a little ear in the corner. One day I started the process as described in step 1 and saw that there was no little ear. So you can choose whether to start in the traditional way or try my way.

1. To begin, weave the yarn through the first stitch on the front needle knitwise and push the stitch off the needle. Then weave the yarn through the next stitch on the front needle purlwise (now the first stitch) and leave it on the needle. Weave the yarn through the first stitch on the back needle purlwise and push the stitch off the needle. Then weave the yarn through the next stitch on the back needle knitwise (now first stitch) and leave it on the needle.

2. Weave the yarn through the first stitch on the front needle knitwise and push that stitch off the needle. Weave the yarn through the next stitch (now first stitch) on the front needle purlwise and leave it on needle.

3. Weave the yarn through the first stitch on the back needle purlwise and push the stitch off the needle. Weave the yarn through the next stitch (now first stitch) on the back needle knitwise and leave it on the needle.

Repeat steps 2 and 3 until there are two stitches left, one in front and one in back. Weave the yarn through the first stitch on the front needle knitwise and then push that stitch off the needle. Weave the yarn through the first stitch on the back needle purlwise and push it off the needle. Pull the tapestry needle and yarn through the sock to the inside and weave in the tail.

Here's the short version.

Begin with:

Front knit off, purl on

Back purl off, knit on

Continue with:

Front knit off, purl on

Back purl off, knit on

End with:

Front knit off

Back purl off

THE KNOT ISSUE

When working on your socks, you may encounter an irregularity or even a knot in your yarn. This seems to hold true especially for hand-dyed yarns. I highly recommend that you cut and restart the yarn past the problem, leaving comfortable tails on both the end and the beginning of the new strand. These tails will be woven in later. If you decide to continue and knit the faulty yarn, it could very well open and unravel later on. Once this happens, there are no tails to fix the weak spot and all your hard work will go into the trash.

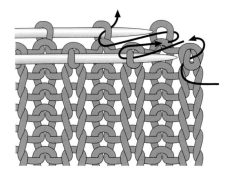

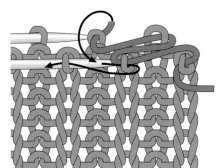

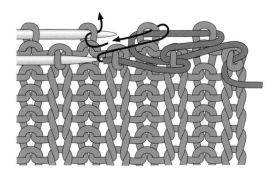

The Basic Sock Pattern

The basic sock pattern is designed to fit a medium foot, right around a woman's size 8 shoe. I wear size 9½ and it still fits me comfortably, although it's snug. If you prefer your socks a little looser, try using size 6 needles for this first project. If your feet are much smaller, try working with size 4 needles. In any case, try your socks on as you work on them. You'll know right away if they fit correctly or if they need to be adjusted.

TIP: For your first pair of socks, consider choosing a light-colored, worsted-weight yarn, which will make it easier for you to see and keep track of the stitches on your needles. For added effect and fun, you can try a lightly variegated or tweed yarn and watch the magic of color spread automatically as you work on your project. I used Cascade 220 Tweed in light gray. I love the way this yarn works up as well as the way it wears. These socks, however, will need to be hand washed because 100% wool will felt and lose its elasticity if machine washed—something to consider when picking your yarn.

MATERIALS

1 skein of Cascade 220 Tweed (90% Peruvian highland wool, 10% Donegal (Tweed); 100 g/3.5 oz; 200 m/220 yds), color 7616. **(4)** Wind 2 even-sized balls from the skein so you have 1 ball for each sock.

Size 5 circular needles (16" and 24")

Point protectors

Stitch markers

Tapestry needle

GAUGE

6 sts = 1" in St st

TIP: If you hate your chronically tight cast on as much as I do, try this: take one end of each circular needle, hold them together, and cast on over *both* needles. When you have the required amount of stitches, simply pull out the 16" needle and voilà! You now have an easy-access cast on and won't have to knit-fight itty-bitty stitches in your first row.

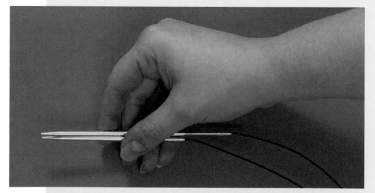

Hold your needles together as one.

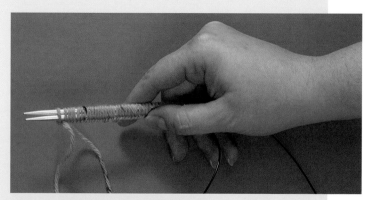

Stitches cast on, using two needles.

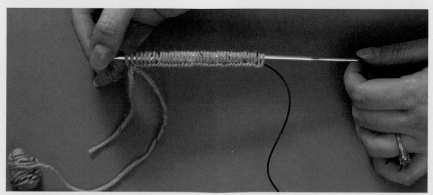

Here are the stitches on the 24" needle after pulling out the 16" needle.

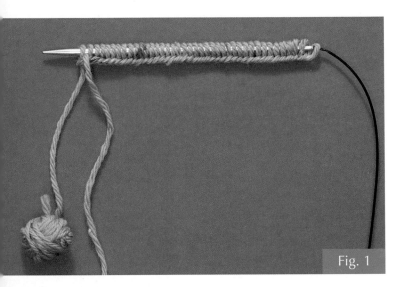
Fig. 1

SETTING UP YOUR CIRCULAR NEEDLES

CO 40 sts for your first sock, using 1 of your 2 balls of yarn and the 24" needle.

After you've CO 40 sts, your work should look like figure 1.

Take the 16" needle and slide half of the sts (20 sts) pw from the 24" needle onto the 16" needle. The working strand of yarn (the one attached to your ball) as well as the open end of your sock should now face away from the needle tips and toward the cables (fig. 2).

Fig. 2

FACT: When I teach my sock workshops, a lot of students ask me which way to slip the stitches from one needle to the other. When you read a pattern and it instructs you to slip one or more stitches without specifying whether to do so as if to knit or as if to purl, you are expected to slip your stitch(es) as if to purl. Unless your pattern tells you specifically to slip the stitches knitwise, you'll always slip them purlwise.

Push all sts simultaneously to the other end of both needles. The working yarn should now hang from the tip of your 16" needle, and the open side of your sock should face the needle ends (fig. 3).

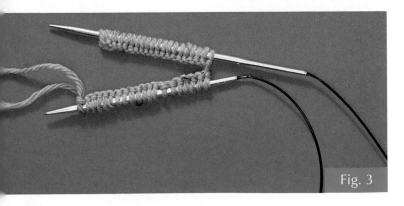
Fig. 3

Let's close the rnd for the first sock. First, you have to make certain that your sts aren't twisted. Take a look at the previous photo and notice how the CO edge faces neatly inward. This is what your work should look like before you join it in the rnd. Thread the tail onto a tapestry needle. Depending on which CO method you used, it will either hang on the same side as your working yarn or on the opposite one. Regardless of where it is, weave the tail through the corresponding (first) st on the opposite side (fig. 4).

Using the tail and the working yarn, tie a tight double knot to close the rnd of sock 1.

For sock 2, use the second ball of yarn and ignore sock 1. If you're worried about losing sts, slide them back closer to the cables or stick point protectors on the tips. Using the 24" needle, or if you used the 2-needle cast-on, go ahead and CO 40 sts, holding the other (empty) ends of your circular needles tog. Pull the 16" needle out of the sts. Your work should look like figure 5.

Use the empty 16" needle tip and slip half of the sts (20 sts) pw onto it. The working yarn as well as the open end of sock 2 should both face away from the needle tips and toward the cables (fig. 6).

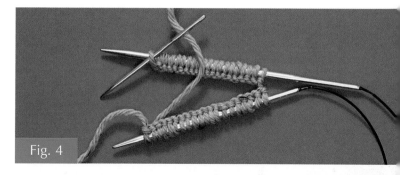

Fig. 4

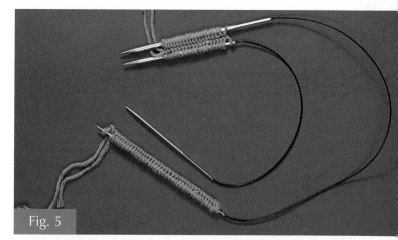

Fig. 5

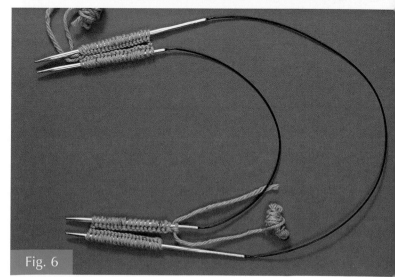

Fig. 6

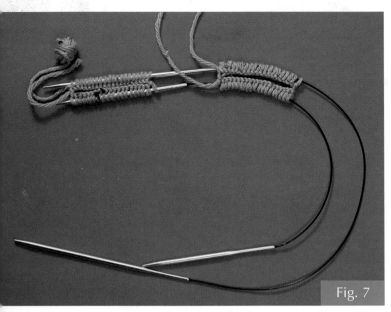

Fig. 7

Hooray! You're now ready to knit the first row and round.

FACT: For many of my students, the hardest concept to understand is the *how* of knitting two socks on circulars; is it a row or is it a round? Well, it's both. Take a look at your work. There are two separate projects on your needles: sock 1 (40 sts) and sock 2 (40 sts). Each sock is divided into two halves; one half (20 sts) sits on the 24" needle and the other half (20 sts) sits on the 16" needle. When you begin to knit, you'll work two halves on one needle, which is a row. When you get to the end of sock 2 on one needle, you turn your work (this is one half of the round), and knit the other two halves of your socks once again in a row. Then you'll turn your work again, thus completing two rows, which equal 1 complete round.

As before, slip the tail onto a tapestry needle and, after making sure your sts are not twisted and the CO edge is facing inward, thread it through the first st of the opposite side. Using the working yarn and the tail, tie a tight double knot to close the gap. Scoot sock 2 along the cables toward sock 1. Your needles and project should look like figure 7.

This is a great time to take a break. Are you running out of time? Do you need to clear your head? It's best to put the socks down and come back to them later if you're unfocused or pressed for time. Otherwise, here we go!

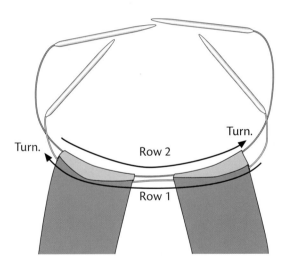

Let's knit the first row (half a rnd) step by step. Before you beg, notice that the needles are parallel and the ends face away from each other. We'll call this arrangement the "row start position." Place a point protector on each end of the 24" needle because you'll be knitting sts on the 16" needle first. Scoot sock 1 of row 1 close to the needle tips and let sock 2 "rest" on the cables. Holding the needles in your left hand with the working yarn at the tips, make sure the 24" needle sits *slightly behind* the 16" one. The working yarn hangs between both needles for sock 1. The strand of yarn for sock 2 should lie over and behind the cable of the 24" needle. This way it will already be set up for later use without getting tangled or accidentally creating an extra st.

Pull the end of the 24" needle to the right and down so that the sts sitting on it slide onto its cable. With your right hand, pick up the empty end of the 16" needle and get ready to knit your first row. Make sure you squeeze the tip of your 16" needle and the cable of the 24" needle tight tog; this will prevent a gap from forming. (fig. 8).

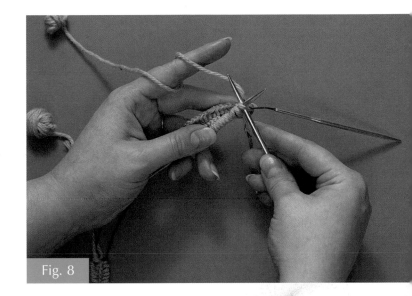
Fig. 8

THE CUFFS

Beg with 20 sts of sock 1: K1, pm, *P1, K1, rep from * to last st, P1.

The stitch marker you've just placed indicates the beginning of the round from now on. Notice how the needle position has changed after you've finished ribbing the first 20 sts. The 16" needle is no longer in its row start position; the tips are now facing each other. This is an excellent reminder that you have not completed the row and that you still have to work 20 sts of cuff for sock 2. Your work should look like figure 9.

Let sock 1 rest and make sure the working yarn hangs behind the 16" needle as well as over and behind the cable of the 24" needle. Scoot the cuff sts of the second sock close to the tip of your needle, making sure the working yarn is picked up straight from the 24" needle and doesn't create an extra st.

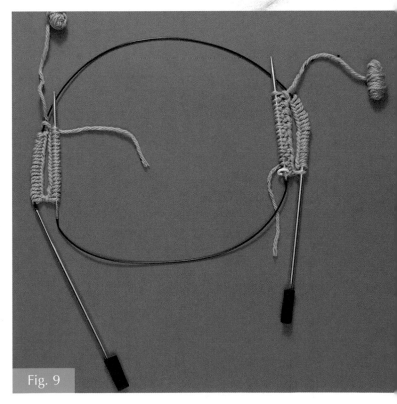
Fig. 9

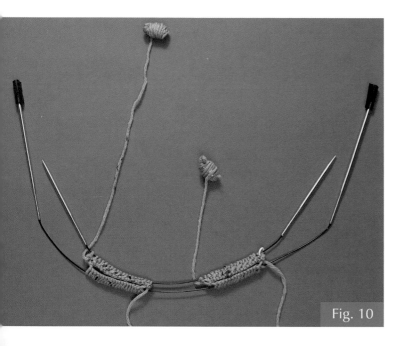

Fig. 10

Again, squeeze the needle tip and cable together to avoid creating a gap. Once more, you'll work K1, P1 ribbing for cuff.

You've just completed 1 row or the first half of a rnd for your socks. Notice how the needles have opened up and lie parallel once again. Looking at your work, you'll see that half of each cuff has been knitted (fig. 10).

To start the second row of the first rnd, turn your work so that the unribbed sts face you, and the needle tips with working yarn attached are in your left hand. This time you'll knit off the 24" needle, so switch the point protectors to the tips of the 16" needle. Remember to switch balls as you switch socks and make sure that the working strand of yarn hangs between the two needles and the resting strand of yarn lies over and behind the back cable.

Align the tips and hold the 16" needle *slightly behind* the 24" one. As before, pull the back needle (16") to the right and forward so its sts slip onto the cable. Squeeze the needle tip (24") and cable (16") close tog to avoid creating a gap, and start the ribbing.

Notice how the tips of the 24" needle face each other after you've worked the cuff for sock 1. Remember that you're only done with half of this row. You still have to knit the cuff for sock 2 to finish the row completely. Once needles are parallel again, you should be ready to start the first row of the next rnd at the st marker.

Hooray! You've finished a complete round for your socks and your needles are once again in the row start position (fig. 11).

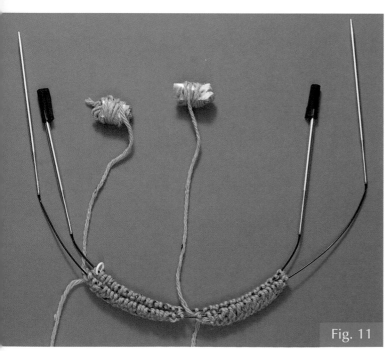

Fig. 11

TIP: In order to tighten the working yarn at the beginning of each set of stitches, try this: knit the first two stitches in pattern, then pause to pull the strand really tight before continuing the row. After knitting the first few rows, it may seem that no matter how tight you pull your yarn, a slight gap remains at each turn. It will disappear completely as long as you remember to continue to knit the first two stitches tightly every time. Should the closing of the round remain uneven, you can always ease it into shape as you weave in your tail at the end.

Depending on your preference, cont to work the cuff in the ribbing for 1½" to 2", using the previous guidelines. The repetitions will help you quickly get the hang of this technique. Remember to switch your point protectors onto the tips of the resting needle. This will help you remember and get used to using the correct needle to knit with. Soon you'll feel confident enough and won't need them anymore (fig. 12).

THE LEGS

After the cuffs have reached the desired length, beg St st on leg (knit every rnd). Here again, you decide the length; how long do you want your sock leg to be (fig. 13)?

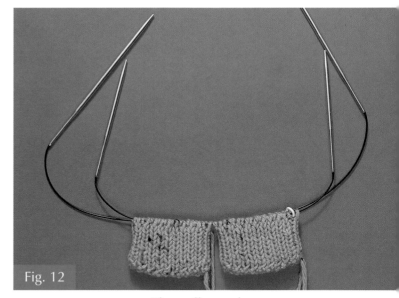

The cuffs are done.

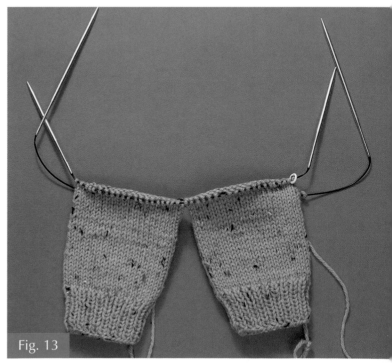

The legs are done.

THE HEEL FLAP

The heel flap is worked in rows on half of the sts (1 needle) only, in this case, the 16" one, which also carries the st marker. To create the flap, you'll no longer knit in rnds but back and forth in rows and St st (knit 1 row, purl 1 row) across both socks. Before you beg, remove the st marker and cover the tips of the 24" needle with point protectors.

For the heel flap, always slip the first st of each set and knit the last one. This will make it easier to see the sts later on when you have to pick them up.

Unless otherwise specified, slip all sts pw.

Row 1 (RS): Sl 1 wyif, *K1, sl 1 wyib, rep from * to last st, K1. Rep for sock 2.

Row 2 (WS): Sl 1 wyif, purl to last st, K1. Rep for sock 2.

Work rows 1 and 2 another 10 times for a total of 22 rows, ending with a completed purl row. Heel flaps should measure 2¼" to 2½" (figs. 14 and 15).

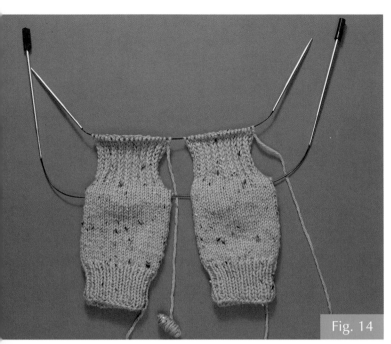

The finished heel flap, right (knit) side.

Fig. 14

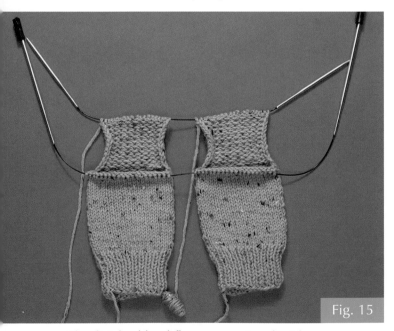

The finished heel flap, wrong (purl) side.

Fig. 15

TIP: To avoid tangling your balls of yarn or accidentally adding stitches, try this: on the right side of the heel flap, knit stitches of sock 1 in pattern and then let your working yarn hang behind the flap, over and behind the cable of the 24" needle. Before beginning the wrong-side row, make sure that the working yarn hanging in the middle lies over and behind the cable of the 16" needle.

On the wrong side of the heel flap, purl stitches of sock 1 in pattern and then let the working yarn hang down toward you, over the cable of the 24" needle. Before beginning the right-side row, make sure the working yarn in the middle remains sitting over the cable of the 24" needle but now hangs *away* from you.

THE HEEL TURN

The heel is turned with the help of short rows, which means that you are going to work back and forth *within* a row rather than completing it. This technique will leave unworked stitches on your needle, and both heels cannot be worked at the same time. Therefore, each heel has to be worked separately as follows:

Sl all sts pw unless otherwise specified.

ITALICIZED INSTRUCTIONS: Note that some of the instructions in the patterns are italicized. This indicates a change of some sort. For example, the first stitch of row 1 (RS) has to be slipped purlwise with the yarn in front to stay true to the side of the heel flap. Once you begin to turn the heel and are working within a row, the first stitch of a right-side row has to be slipped knitwise with the yarn in back. A similar rule applies to the last stitch on the wrong-side rows. As long as you're working within a row, the last stitch gets purled, but when you get to the last wrong-side row, you'll have to knit the last stitch to accommodate the end stitch of the heel flap.

FIRST SOCK

Row 1 (RS): Sl 1 wyif, K10, K2tog, K1, turn.

Row 2 (WS): Sl 1 wyif, P3, ssp, P1, turn.

Row 3: Sl 1 *kw wyib*, K4, K2tog, K1, turn.

Row 4: Sl 1 wyif, P5, ssp, P1, turn.

Row 5: Sl 1 kw wyib, K6, K2tog, K1, turn.

Row 6: Sl 1 wyif, P7, ssp, P1, turn.

Row 7: Sl 1 kw wyib, K8, K2tog, K1, turn.

Row 8: Sl 1 wyif, P9, ssp, *K1*, turn.

Row 9: Sl 1 *wyif*, knit to end of row. *Do not turn your work*—12 sts rem.

GUSSET STITCH

In her book *Sensational Knitted Socks*, Charlene Schurch shows a wonderful way to avoid the most hated gap or hole, which seems to plague gussets and sock knitters all over the world. I've modified this step a little to suit my knitting needs and it works perfectly.

Look closely at the gusset corner and find the last horizontal bar that connects an instep stitch with a heel-flap stitch. To close the gap, pick up both stitches by inserting your knitting needle into the heel-flap stitch from front to back and then into the instep stitch from back to front. You now have both stitches sitting on your right-hand needle. Knit them together, thus creating the extra corner stitch. Follow these directions for picking up one stitch wherever you see "PU 1 gusset st."

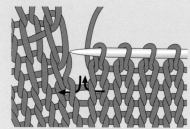

Picking up stitches
when both were knit

The first heel is turned. You should have 12 sts left on your needle. Cont with the *same needle tip*, PU 11 sts along the left side of the heel flap, thus creating the gusset. Then PU 1 st (the 12th st) in the corner of your gusset. See "Gusset Stitch" above.

After you've picked up and knitted a total of 12 gusset sts, this sock gets to rest while you work on turning the heel of sock 2 (fig. 16).

Before you beg on the second heel, notice that the tips of your 16" needle are facing each other; the row is only half completed. Move sock 1 off the RH needle and onto the cable. Pick up the needle that holds the second heel in your left hand and turn the heel as follows:

SECOND SOCK

Row 1 (RS): Sl 1 wyif, K10, K2tog, K1, turn.

Row 2 (WS): Sl 1 wyif, P3, ssp, P1, turn.

Row 3: Sl 1 *kw wyib*, K4, K2tog, K1, turn.

Row 4: Sl 1 wyif, P5, ssp, P1, turn.

Row 5: Sl 1 kw wyib, K6, K2tog, K1, turn.

Row 6: Sl 1 wyif, P7, ssp, P1, turn.

Row 7: Sl 1 kw wyib, K8, K2tog, K1, turn.

Row 8: Sl 1 wyif, P9, ssp, *K1*, turn.

Row 9: Sl 1 *wyif*, knit to end of row. *Do not turn your work.*

You've just turned the second heel and once again you should have 12 sts left on your needle. Cont with the *same needle tip* you just worked with, PU 11 sts along the side of the heel flap, then PU 1 gusset st in the corner as before (fig. 17).

One heel has been turned and 12 gusset stitches have been picked up.

Both heels have been turned and two sets of gusset stitches have been picked up.

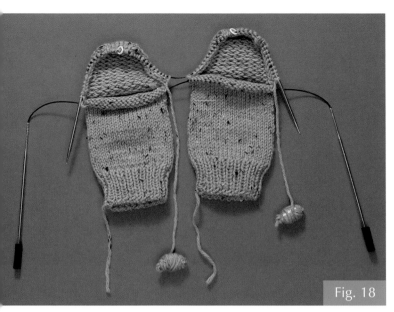

Both heels have been turned and all gusset stitches have been picked up.

Turn your work so that 40 instep sts are facing you (20 sts per sock). Switch the point protectors to the 16" needle and knit even across instep sts for both socks, using the 24" needle. Remember to push the sts of sock 1 back onto the cable so you'll be able to tighten the working yarn after the second st. Turn.

The heel sts are facing you once again. Switch the point protectors to the 24" needle. You'll now pick up and knit gusset sts on the second side of sock 1, this time starting at the gusset corner and working up the heel flap. With your LH, pick up the corresponding left side of the 16" needle. Move it into your RH and grab the heel flap to be worked in your LH. The working yarn should be ready and waiting in the corner of the gusset of this sock.

PU 1 gusset st in the corner as before. Pull the working yarn tight and cont to PU 11 more sts along the side of the heel flap. After all sts have been picked up, you should be at the heel. Knit across the first 6 heel sts and pm. Cont to knit across the rem heel sts as well as the previously picked-up gusset sts on the other side. After you're done with sock 1, push it away from the tip and onto the cable of the 16" needle.

Using the second ball and the needle you're currently holding in your RH, PU 1 gusset st in the corner of sock 2. Pull the working yarn nice and tight and cont to PU 11 more sts along the side of the heel flap. Knit across the first 6 heel sts and pm. Cont to knit across the rem heel sts as well as the previously picked-up gusset sts on the other side. The 2 st markers will help you check your work and dec evenly in the next step (fig. 18).

Both heels are turned and all gusset sts have been picked up. From now on, you'll once again knit in rows as well as rnds. If you still need a little help remembering, cont to switch point protectors to the tips of the resting needle.

GUSSET DECREASES AND WORKING THE FOOT

Take a look at your work. The 24" needle is holding the 40 instep sts (20 sts per sock). The 16" needle is holding the sole and gusset sts, a total of 72 sts (36 sts per sock).

Turn your work so the instep sts are facing you and knit across them. Turn the work so the sole sts are facing you. From now on, you'll knit even across the instep sts and dec gusset sts on the 16" needle until there are once again 20 sts per sole. Work the dec of the gusset sts as shown on page 33.

Rnd 1

Row 1 (sole): Knit across sock 1 to last 3 sts, K2tog, K1. Rep for sock 2.

Row 2 (instep): Knit even across instep sts of both socks.

Rnd 2

Row 1 (sole): K1, ssk, knit to end of sock 1. Rep for sock 2.

Row 2 (instep): Knit even across instep sts of both socks.

Rep rnds 1 and 2 until the original number of sts, a total of 40 sts per sock, rem (20 sts per half). Remove 1 st marker and leave 1 to mark the needle that starts the rnd.

Once you've reached 20 sts per sole, work the feet of the socks in St st (knit each rnd) until the foot measures 8" from the back of the heel, or until it reaches the base of your big toe when the sock is tried on (fig. 19).

THE SHAPED TOE

The shaped toe is done by dec on both sides of the foot, 2 sts on the sole side and 2 sts on the instep side, for a total of 4 sts on EOR. You should be ready to beg dec on the sole side (16" needle).

Rnd 1

Rows 1 (sole) and 2 (instep): K1, ssk, knit to last 3 sts of sock 1, K2tog, K1. Rep for sock 2.

Rnd 2: Knit even across both needles.

Rep rnds 1 and 2 until a total of 20 sts rem per sock (10 sts per half), ending with rnd 2.

Rep rnd 1 until a total of 12 sts rem per sock (6 sts per half).

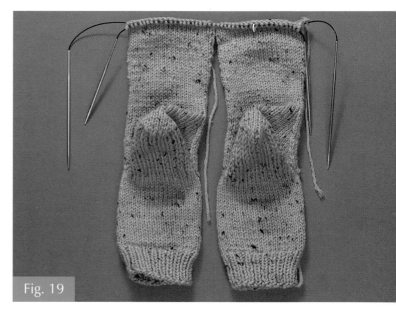

Fig. 19

Work until the foot reaches 8" or the base of the big toe.

Cut yarn for both socks, leaving a generous tail (7" to 10").

GRAFTING THE TOE

To close the toe without a seam, you'll work with both needles (instep and sole sts) at the same time for each sock. Push all sts for sock 1 close to the ends of both needles and hold them in your LH. As before, one needle will sit behind the other, and the front one should sit slightly lower than the back one. The working yarn should be attached to the needle held in back (in this case, 24" needle). Weave the toe sts tog with kitchener st (see page 18).

Weave in all ends and *immediately* try your socks on! Congratulations! You've just finished your first pair of socks on two circular needles. Now turn the page and find more awesome patterns to make.

*C*hunky, cozy cotton socks

I usually don't like to knit socks with cotton because it lacks the springiness a sock needs to mold itself comfortably around my leg and foot and stay there. Enter Patagonia Nature Cotton by Araucania Yarns, a chunky thick-and-thin yarn that is supersoft and cozy. It has certainly stolen this knitter's heart.

Due to low blood pressure, my feet are perpetually frozen, no matter the time of year. In the winter, I shuffle through the house wearing kitschy, fluffy pink slippers or my UGGs, which keep my feet nice and warm. In the summertime, I play the on-again/off-again game with any sort of shoe or woolen sock in the house, and my feet are either sweaty and icky or icy cold. Cotton breathes, so it won't overheat your feet. At the same time, it keeps them warm, not toasty and sweaty, the perfect all-natural fiber for my summer house socks.

Sizes: Small (Medium, Large)
To fit shoe size: 5-6 (7-9, 10-11)

MATERIALS

2 skeins of Patagonia Nature Cotton from Araucania Yarns (100% cotton; 100 g/3.5 oz; 105 yds/100 m), color 210 (**5**)

Size 8 circular needles (16" and 24")

Point protectors

Stitch markers

Tapestry needle

GAUGE

4 sts = 1" in St st

TIP: To avoid confusion, circle or highlight the appropriate instructions for the size sock you are making.

CUFFS/LEG

CO 28 (32, 32) sts per sock and set up needles as for "The Basic Sock Pattern" (page 20). You should be ready to start with your 16" needle.

Knit in K2, P2 ribbing for 6" or until desired length.

Small and Large: Knit 2 rows even.

Medium: Knit 1 row and AT SAME TIME dec 2 sts evenly in each half sock, for a total of 4 sts per sock—28 sts rem per sock.

NOTE: For the pattern to work correctly, begin and end stitches as follows:

Small and Medium: Beg and end each set of 14 sts on your 16" needle with K2 (14 is not divisible by 4). Beg and end each set of 14 sts on 24" needle with P2.

Large: Beg each set of sts on both needles with K2 and end with P2 since the 16 sts per set (32 per sock) are divisible by 4.

HEEL FLAP

The heel flap is worked in rows on half of the sts (1 needle) only. To help you remember which needle, place point protectors on the "resting needle" (24") before you beg. Remove st marker.

Unless otherwise specified, slip all sts pw.

Row 1 (RS): Sl 1 wyif, *K1, sl 1 wyib, rep from * to last st, K1. Rep for sock 2.

Row 2 (WS): Sl 1 wyif, purl to last st, K1. Rep for sock 2.

Rep rows 1 and 2 until heel flap measures 2¼ (2½, 2½)".

TURNING THE HEEL

The heel is turned with the help of short rows; there-fore, each heel is worked separately, beg with sock 1. Cont to work with 16" needles and keep point protectors on 24" needles.

NOTE: After knitting sock 1 on the right-side row, let the working yarn hang behind the flap, over and behind the cable of 24" needle. Then fling the same strand over and behind the 16" needle before starting the wrong-side row.

After knitting sock 1 on the wrong-side row, let the working yarn hang over the cable of 24" needle and toward you. Make sure that the same strand continues to hang over the cable of 24" needle (now away from you) before starting on the right-side row.

ALL SIZES

Row 1 (RS): Sl 1 pw wyif, K7 (7, 8), K2tog, K1, turn.

Row 2 (WS): Sl 1 pw wyif, P3, ssp, P1, turn.

Row 3: Sl 1 *kw wyib*, K4, K2tog, K1, turn.

Row 4: Sl 1 pw wyif, P5, ssp, P1, turn.

SMALL AND MEDIUM

Row 5 (RS): Sl 1 *kw wyib*, K6, K2tog, turn.

Row 6: Sl 1 pw wyif, P6, ssp, turn.

Row 7: Sl 1 pw wyif, K7, *do not turn*—8 sts rem.

LARGE

Row 5 (RS): Sl 1 *kw wyib*, K6, K2tog, K1, turn.

Row 6: Sl 1 pw wyif, P6, ssp, *K1*, turn.

Row 7: Sl 1 *pw wyif*, K9, *do not turn*—10 sts rem.

For all sizes, cont with same needle tip, PU 9 (9, 10) sts alongside heel flap, PU 1 gusset st in corner for a total of 10 (10, 11) sts. Move this sock onto the cable and cont with same needle tip, turn heel of sock 2 as for sock 1.

After second heel is turned, cont with same needle tip, PU 9 (9, 10) sts along side of heel flap, PU 1 gusset st in corner for a total of 10 (10, 11) sts. Turn. If necessary, switch point protectors to appropriate needle.

Knit even across all instep sts. Turn.

Beg in gusset corner of sock 1, *PU 1 gusset st in corner, PU 9 (9, 10) sts along second side of heel flap for a total of 10 (10, 11) sts. K4 (4, 5) heel sts, pm, knit across rem heel and gusset sts on other side. Rep from * for sock 2, beg in gusset corner. Turn.

Knit even across all instep sts. Turn.

Both heels are turned and all gusset sts have been picked up. From now on, you'll once again knit in rows as well as rnds.

Patagonia has such wonderful colorways, it's hard to decide which one to use. This is color 212.

GUSSET DECREASES AND WORKING THE FOOT

Only sole sts are dec (16" needle).

Rnd 1

Row 1 (sole): Knit across to last 3 sts, K2tog, K1. Rep for sock 2.

Row 2 (instep): Knit even across both socks.

Rnd 2

Row 1 (sole): K1, ssk, knit to end. Rep for sock 2.

Row 2 (instep): Knit even across both socks.

Rep rnds 1 and 2 until there are 14 (14, 16) sole sts left per sock, matching number of instep sts for a total of 28 (28, 32) sts per sock.

Remove 1 st marker and leave 1 to mark the needle that starts the rnd. Knit even across sole and instep sts until foot measures approx 7 (8, 8½)" from back of heel, or until it reaches the base of your big toe when sock is tried on.

SHAPED TOE

Beg dec with sole sts (16" needle).

Rnd 1

Rows 1 (sole) and 2 (instep): K1, ssk, knit to last 3 sts, K2tog, K1. Rep for sock 2.

Rnd 2: Knit even across both needles.

Rep rnds 1 and 2 until 8 total sts rem per sock, 4 sts per half.

Cut yarn for both socks, leaving a generous tail (7" to 10").

Use kitchener st to graft toe sts tog for each sock (see page 18).

Anne's magic stripes

All the exquisite yarns available today positively spoil me, and having to choose which ones to use for my patterns was not an easy task by any means. Self-striping sock yarns are extremely popular and tons of fun. They come in many fiber blends and color combinations, and all we have to do is knit round and round and let the yarn do its magic. For this basic stripe pattern, I picked lovely Anne, daughter of Schaefer Yarn, which is home to many superb hand-painted luxury fibers, and one of my favorites. Enjoy.

Sizes: Small (Medium, Large)
To fit shoe size: 5-6 (7-9, 10-11)

MATERIALS

1 skein of Anne from Schaefer Yarn (60% merino wool Superwash, 25% mohair, 15% nylon; 4 oz; 560 yds)

Size 2 circular needles (16" and 24")

Point protectors

Stitch markers

Tapestry needle

GAUGE

7½ sts = 1" in St st

CUFFS

CO and set up 56 (64, 64) sts per sock.

Work in K1, P1 ribbing for 1" or until desired length.

LEGS

Work in St st until leg measures 7" or desired length.

In last rnd, evenly dec 2 (2, 0) sts per half sock for a total of 4 (4, 0) sts per sock—52 (60, 64) sts rem.

HEEL FLAP

The heel flap is worked in rows on half of the sts (1 needle) only. To help you remember which needle, place point protectors on resting needle before you beg. Remove st marker.

Unless otherwise specified, sl all sts pw.

Row 1 (RS): Sl 1 wyif, *K1, sl 1 wyib, rep from * to last st, K1. Rep for sock 2.

Row 2 (WS): Sl 1 wyif, purl to last st, K1. Rep for sock 2.

Rep rows 1 and 2 until heel flap measures 2¼ (2½, 2½)".

TURNING THE HEEL

The heel is turned with the help of short rows; therefore, each heel is worked separately, beg with sock 1. Cont to work in rows and with same needle as for heel flap.

Unless otherwise specified, sl all sts pw.

ALL SIZES

Row 1 (RS): Sl 1 wyif, K14 (16, 16), K2tog, K1, turn.

Row 2 (WS): Sl 1 wyif, P5 (5, 3), ssp, P1, turn.

Row 3: Sl 1 *kw wyib*, K6 (6, 4), K2tog, K1, turn.

Row 4: Sl 1 wyif, P7 (7, 5), ssp, P1, turn.

Row 5: Sl 1 kw wyib, K8 (8, 6), K2tog, K1, turn.

Row 6: Sl 1 wyif, P9 (9, 7), ssp, P1, turn.

Row 7: Sl 1 kw wyib, K10 (10, 8), K2tog, K1, turn.

Row 8: Sl 1 wyif, P11 (11, 9), ssp, P1, turn.

Row 9: Sl 1 kw wyib, K12 (12, 10), K2tog, K1, turn.

SMALL

Row 10: Sl 1 wyif, P13, ssp, *K1*, turn.

Row 11: Sl 1 *pw wyif*, K15, *do not turn—16 sts rem.*

MEDIUM

Row 10: Sl 1 wyif, P13, ssp, *K1*, turn.

Row 11: Sl 1 kw wyib, K14, K2tog, K1, turn.

Row 12: Sl 1 wyif, P15, ssp, *K1*, turn.

Row 13: Sl 1 *pw wyif*, K17, *do not turn—18 sts rem.*

LARGE

Row 10: Sl 1 wyif, P11, ssp, P1, turn.

Row 11: Sl 1 kw wyib, K12, K2tog, K1, turn.

Row 12: Sl 1 wyif, P13, ssp, P1, turn.

Row 13: Sl 1 kw wyib, K14, K2tog, K1, turn.

Row 14: Sl 1 wyif, ssp, P15, *K1*, turn.

Row 15: Sl 1 *pw wyif*, K17, *do not turn—18 sts rem.*

For all sizes, cont with same needle tip, PU 16 (18, 18) sts along heel flap, PU 1 gusset st in corner for a total of 17 (19, 19) sts. Move sock to cable and turn heel for sock 2 as for sock 1. After second heel is turned, cont with same needle tip, PU 16 (18, 18) sts along heel flap, PU 1 gusset st in corner for a total of 17 (19, 19) sts. Turn. If necessary, switch point protectors to appropriate needle.

Knit even across all instep sts (24" needle). Turn.

Beg at gusset corner of sock 1, *PU 1 gusset st in corner, then PU 16 (18, 18) sts along second side of heel flap. K8 (9, 9) heel sts, pm, knit across rem heel and gusset sts on other side. Rep from * for sock 2, beg in gusset corner. Turn.

Knit even across all instep sts. Turn.

Both heels are turned and all gusset sts have been picked up. From now on, you'll once again knit in rows as well as rnds. If you still need a little help remembering, cont to switch point protectors to tips of resting needle.

GUSSET DECREASES AND WORKING THE FOOT

Only sole sts are dec.

Rnd 1

Row 1 (sole): Knit across to last 3 sts, K2tog, K1. Rep for sock 2.

Row 2 (instep): Knit even across both socks.

Rnd 2

Row 1 (sole): K1, ssk, knit to end. Rep for sock 2.

Row 2 (instep): Knit even across both socks.

Rep rnds 1 and 2 until there are 26 (30, 32) sole sts left per sock, matching number of instep sts for a total of 52 (60, 64) sts per sock.

Remove 1 st marker and leave 1 to mark the needle that starts the rnd. Knit even across sole and instep sts until foot measures approx 7 (7½, 8)" from back of heel, or until it reaches the base of your big toe when sock is tried on.

SHAPED TOE

These socks have a more rounded toe due to a change in the dec sequence. I like them a lot, especially since they don't end up pointy and strange looking. Give it a try and see how you like this method; you can always revert to the more traditional technique of dec EOR.

For all sizes, beg dec with sole sts (16" needle).

Rnd 1

Rows 1 (sole) and 2 (instep): K1, ssk, knit to last 3 sts, K2tog, K1. Rep for sock 2.

Rnds 2–4: Knit even across both needles.

Rnd 5

Rows 1 and 2: K1, ssk, knit to last 3 sts, K2tog, K1. Rep for sock 2.

Rnds 6 and 7: Knit even across both needles.

Rnd 8

Rows 1 and 2: K1, ssk, knit to last 3 sts, K2tog, K1. Rep for sock 2.

Rnds 9 and 10: Knit even across both needles.

Rnd 11

Rows 1 and 2: K1, ssk, knit to last 3 sts, K2tog, K1. Rep for sock 2.

Rnd 12: Knit even across both needles.

Rnd 13

Rows 1 and 2: K1, ssk, knit to last 3 sts, K2tog, K1. Rep for sock 2.

Rnd 14: Knit even across both needles.

Rnd 15

Rows 1 and 2: K1, ssk, knit to last 3 sts, K2tog, K1. Rep for sock 2.

Rnd 16: Knit even across both needles.

Rep rnd 15 only until 12 (16, 16) total sts rem per sock.

Cut yarn for both socks, leaving a generous tail (7 to 10)".

Use kitchener st to graft toe sts tog for each sock (see page 18).

Beads create instant elegance and sparkle, and there are lots of ways to work them into your projects. I've chosen two different methods for you to try. Some beads are actually knit into the sock, but the majority are hand sewn on top. It's easier this way to place them exactly where you want them, and because they are sitting on the outside of the sock, you won't run the risk of having them irritate your skin. Finally, it's easier to exchange a damaged bead by cutting the thread rather than having to use pliers to break the bead itself. Beware! Working with beads *is* addictive, and you may soon find yourself adding glitz to many other projects.

Sizes: Small (Medium, Large)
To fit shoe size: 5-6 (7-9, 10-11)

MATERIALS

2 skeins of Regia Silk from Schachenmayr (55% new wool, 20% silk, 25% polyamide; 50 g/1.75 oz; 200 m/210 yds), color 005

Small: Size 1 circular needles (16" and 24")

Medium: Size 2 circular needles (16" and 24")

Large: Size 3 circular needles (16" and 24")

72 beads, size 6 (4 mm), or beads sized to fit yarn

Beading needle

Nylon upholstery thread that matches yarn

10" x 10" piece of felt

Point protectors

Stitch markers

Tapestry needle

GAUGE

Small: 7¾ sts = 1" in St st on size 1 needles

Medium: 7 sts = 1" in St st on size 2 needles

Large: 6¼ sts = 1" in St st on size 3 needles

SPECIAL INSTRUCTIONS

PUB: Pull up bead and snuggle it close to knitting needle.

Star: P3tog, but do not sl sts off LH needle, YO, purl through same 3 sts on LH needle (you've created 3 new sts on RH needle), now sl 3 sts off LH needle.

NOTE: Before you cast on stitches you have to prestring six beads onto the working yarn. Lay a swatch of felt on a table and gently pour a small amount of beads onto it. Thread the beading needle with the working yarn, and pick up 6 beads with the needle. Then slide them over the needle and onto the yarn. Repeat for second sock.

CUFFS

Using appropriate-size needles for your sock size, CO and set up 60 sts for each sock, working with prestrung beads as follows: Push beads close to skein (away from tail end of yarn). Using long-tail CO and *making sure tail end lies over thumb,* *CO 10 sts, PUB, rep from * until 60 sts have been CO. The last bead will sit under your needle unsecured until you close the rnd for the sock.

The 16" needle represents the start of the rnd.

Work in K1, P1 ribbing for 1¼" or desired length.

LEGS

Work star patt as follows:

Rnds 1–4 (8 rows): Knit.

Rnd 5
Row 1: K1, pm, star, *K7, star, rep from * to last 6 sts, K6. Rep for sock 2.

Row 2: K1, star, *K7, star, rep from * to last 6 sts, K6. Rep for sock 2.

Rnds 6–9: Knit.

Rnd 10
Row 1: K6, star, *K7, star, rep from * to last st, K1. Rep for sock 2.

Row 2: K6, star, *K7, star, rep from * to last st, K1. Rep for sock 2.

Rep rnds 1–10 twice more. For a longer/shorter leg length, adjust the number of times you rep rnds 1–10 (rnds 1–10 = approx 1"). Work rnds 1–7 once more, and then work rnds 8 and 9 as follows:

Rnd 8
Row 1: K4, K2tog, knit to last 6 sts, K2tog, K4. Rep for sock 2.

Row 2: K4, K2tog, knit to last 6 sts, K2tog, K4. Rep for sock 2—56 total sts per sock.

Rnd 9: Knit.
Leg will measure 4½" from CO edge.

HEEL FLAP

The heel flap is worked in rows on half of sts (1 needle) only. To help you remember which needle, place point protectors on resting needle before you beg. Remove st marker.

Unless otherwise specified, sl all sts pw.

Row 1 (RS): Sl 1 wyif, *K1, sl 1 wyib, rep from * to last st, K1.

Row 2 (WS): Sl 1 wyif, purl to last st, K1.

Work rows 1 and 2 another 15 times for a total of 32 rows, ending with a completed purl row. Heel measures 2¼".

TURNING THE HEEL

The heel is turned with the help of short rows; therefore, each heel is worked separately, beg with sock 1. Cont to work in rows and with same needle as for heel flap.

Unless otherwise specified, sl all sts pw.

Row 1 (RS): Sl 1 wyif, K15, K2tog, K1, turn.

Row 2 (WS): Sl 1 wyif, P5, ssp, P1, turn.

Row 3: Sl 1 *kw wyib*, K6, K2tog, K1, turn.

Row 4: Sl 1 wyif, P7, ssp, P1, turn.

Row 5: Sl 1 kw wyib, K8, K2tog, K1, turn.

Row 6: Sl 1 wyif, P9, ssp, P1, turn.

Row 7: Sl 1 kw wyib, K10, K2tog, K1, turn.

Row 8: Sl 1 wyif, P11, ssp, P1, turn.

Row 9: Sl 1 kw wyib, K12, K2tog, K1, turn.

Row 10: Sl 1 wyif, P13, ssp, P1, turn.

Row 11: Sl 1 kw wyib, K14, K2tog, turn.

Row 12: Sl 1 wyif, P14, ssp, turn.

Row 13: Sl 1 *pw wyif,* K15, *do not turn*—16 sts rem.

For all sizes, cont with same needle tip, PU 16 sts along heel flap, PU 1 gusset st in corner for a total of 17 sts. Move sock to cable and turn heel of sock 2 as for sock 1.

After second heel is turned, cont with same needle tip, PU 16 sts along heel flap, PU 1 gusset st in corner for a total of 17 sts. Turn. If necessary, switch point protectors appropriately.

For sock 1, *knit across 28 instep sts in star patt as follows: K5, star, K7, star, K6, star, K1. Rep from * for sock 2, turn.

Beg in gusset corner of sock 1, **PU 1 gusset st in corner, then PU 16 sts along second side of heel flap. K8 heel sts and pm, knit across rem heel and gusset sts on other side. Rep from ** for sock 2, beg at gusset corner. Turn.

Knit even across all instep sts. Turn.

Both heels are turned and all gusset sts have been picked up. From now on, you'll once again knit in rows as well as rnds. If you still need a little help remembering, cont to switch point protectors to tips of resting needle.

GUSSET DECREASES AND WORKING THE FOOT

Only sole sts are dec.

Rnd 1

Row 1 (sole): Knit across to last 3 sts, K2tog, K1. Rep for sock 2.

Row 2 (instep): Knit even across both socks.

Rnd 2

Row 1 (sole): K1, ssk, knit to end of sock. Rep for sock 2.

Row 2 (instep): Knit even across both socks.

Rnd 3

Row 1 (sole): Knit across to last 3 sts, K2tog, K1. Rep for sock 2.

Row 2 (instep): Knit even across both socks.

Rnd 4

Row 1 (sole): K1, ssk, knit to end of sock. Rep for sock 2.

Row 2 (instep): K1, star, *K6, star, rep from *, K5. Rep for sock 2.

Rnd 5

Row 1 (sole): Knit across to last 3 sts, K2tog, K1. Rep for sock 2.

Row 2 (instep): Knit even across both socks.

Rnd 6

Row 1 (sole): K1, ssk, knit to end of sock. Rep for sock 2.

Row 2 (instep): Knit even across both socks, turn.

Rnd 7

Row 1 (sole): Knit across to last 3 sts, K2tog, K1. Rep for sock 2.

Row 2 (instep): Knit even across both socks.

Rnd 8

Row 1 (sole): K1, ssk, knit to end of sock. Rep for sock 2.

Row 2 (instep): Knit even across both socks.

Rnd 9

Row 1 (sole): Knit across to last 3 sts, K2tog, K1. Rep for sock 2.

Row 2 (instep): K5, star, K7, star, K6, star, K1. Rep for sock 2.

Rnd 10

Row 1 (sole): K1, ssk, knit to end of sock. Rep for sock 2.

Row 2 (instep): Knit even across both socks.

Rep rnds 1–10 until 28 sole sts rem per sock—total of 56 sts per sock.

Remove 1 st marker and leave 1 to mark the needle that starts the rnd. Rep rnds 1–10, knitting even across sole sts without dec and in star patt across instep sts until foot measures approx 7 (7½, 8)" from back of heel, or until it reaches the base of your big toe when sock is tried on.

SHAPED TOE

Beg dec with sole sts (16" needle).

Rnd 1

Rows 1 (sole) and 2 (instep): K1, ssk, knit to last 3 sts, K2tog, K1. Rep for sock 2.

Rnd 2: Knit even across both needles.

Rep rnds 1 and 2 until 14 total sts rem per sock—7 sts per half.

Rep rnd 1 until 10 total sts rem per sock—5 sts per half.

Cut yarn for both socks, leaving a generous tail (7 to 10").

Use kitchener st to graft toe sts tog for each sock (see page 18).

SEWING ON BEADS

Sew beads onto stars of first 5 patt rnds from top of leg down. Adding beads to any more rnds may cause beads to sit inside your shoe and rub your ankles or feet. I put my beads on top of the star patt, making them look like little shooting stars. Feel free to experiment with the position of your beads to see what you like best.

Take your beading needle or a sewing needle that is thin enough to slide through bead hole, thread it with upholstery thread, and pull it through sock fabric from the inside out. Pick up and slide a bead down thread until it sits on top of sock. Take needle and pull it back through sock from outside in; make sure you like the position of your bead, tightly double or triple knot the thread, and cut, leaving short little ends. Don't worry; you can't feel the thread at all when you are wearing your socks.

Silver pearls are stunning on a dark canvas. Here the pattern is shown in Regia Silk Shine in color 150.

Cabled corn

Sometimes I wonder if after all these years of obsessive knitting, I might get bored with yarns and patterns because the "yarn people" have finally run out of ideas. Enter Cornucopia by Kolláge Yarns, which is made of 100% corn, and suddenly I know in my little knitter's heart that they will continue to research, design, and create fibers to make even the most serious knitter giggle with utter excitement.

Sizes: Small (Medium, Large)
To fit shoe size: 5-6 (7-9, 10-11)

MATERIALS

3 (3, 4) skeins of Cornucopia from Kolláge Yarns (100% corn; 34 g; 100 yds), color Island Sea (❸)

Size 3 circular needles (16" and 24")

Cable needle

Point protectors

Stitch markers

Stitch holders or waste yarn

Tapestry needle

GAUGE

7 sts = 1" in St st

CUFFS

CO and set up 48 (52, 56) sts per sock.

Work in K1, P1 ribbing for 1½" or desired length.

LEGS

C6B: Sl 3 sts to cn; hold at back; K3, K3 from cn.

Rnd 1
Rows 1 and 2: K1, (P1, K1) 2 (2, 3) times, P0 (1, 0), pm, K2, P2, K6, P2, K2, pm, P0 (1, 0), (K1, P1) 2 (2, 3) times, K1. Rep for sock 2.

Rnd 2
Rows 1 and 2: K1, (K1, P1) 2 (2, 3) times, K2 (3, 2), P2, K6, P2, K2 (3, 2), (P1, K1) 2 (2, 3) times, K1. Rep for sock 2.

Rnd 3 and all odd-numbered rnds
Rows 1 and 2: K1, (P1, K1) 2 (2, 3) times, K2 (3, 2), P2, K6, P2, K2 (3, 2), (K1, P1) 2 (2, 3) times, K1. Rep for sock 2.

Rnd 4

Rows 1 and 2: K1, (K1, P1) 2 (2, 3) times, K2 (3, 2), P2, C6B, P2, K2 (3, 2), (P1, K1) 2 (2, 3) times, K1. Rep for sock 2.

Rnd 6: As rnd 2.

Rnd 8

Rows 1 and 2: K1, (K1, P1) 2 (2, 3) times, K2 (3, 2), P2, K1, YO, K2tog, K3, P2, K2 (3, 2), (P1, K1) 2 (2, 3) times, K1. Rep for sock 2.

Rnd 10

Rows 1 and 2: K1, (K1, P1) 2 (2, 3) times, K2 (3, 2), P2, sl 1 kw, K1, psso, YO, K4, P2, K2 (3, 2), (P1, K1) 2 (2, 3) times, K1. Rep for sock 2.

Rnd 12

Rows 1 and 2: K1, (K1, P1) 2 (2, 3) times, K2 (3, 2), P2, K1, YO, K2tog, K3, P2, K2 (3, 2), (P1, K1) 2 (2, 3) times, K1. Rep for sock 2.

Rnd 14

Rows 1 and 2: K1, (K1, P1) 2 (2, 3) times, K2 (3, 2), P2, K6, P2, K2 (3, 2), (P1, K1) 2 (2, 3) times, K1. Rep for sock 2.

Rnd 16

Rows 1 and 2: K1, (K1, P1) 2 (2, 3) times, K2 (3, 2), P2, C6B, P2, K2 (3, 2), (P1, K1) 2 (2, 3) times, K1. Rep for sock 2.

Rnd 18

Rows 1 and 2: K1, (K1, P1) 2 (2, 3) times, K2 (3, 2), P2, K6, P2, K2 (3, 2), (P1, K1) 2 (2, 3) times, K1. Rep for sock 2.

Rnd 20

Rows 1 and 2: K1, (K1, P1) 2 (2, 3) times, K2 (3, 2), P2, K3, sl 1 kw, K1, psso, YO, K1, P2, K2 (3, 2), (P1, K1) 2 (2, 3) times, K1. Rep for sock 2.

Rnd 22

Rows 1 and 2: K1, (K1, P1) 2 (2, 3) times, K2 (3, 2), P2, K4, YO, K2tog, P2, K2 (3, 2), (P1, K1) 2 (2, 3) times, K1. Rep for sock 2.

Rnd 24

Rows 1 and 2: K1, (K1, P1) 2 (2, 3) times, K2 (3, 2), P2, K3, sl 1 kw, K1, psso, YO, K1, P2, K2 (3, 2), (P1, K1) 2 (2, 3) times, K1. Rep for sock 2.

Rep rnds 1–24 once more. Then cont as follows:

Rnd 1

Rows 1 and 2: K1, (P1, K1) 2 (2, 3) times, P0 (1, 0), K2tog, P2, K6, P2, K2tog, P0 (1, 0), (K1, P1) 2 (2, 3) times, K1. Rep for sock 2, turn—44 (48, 52) sts per sock.

Rnd 2

Rows 1 and 2: K1, (K1, P1) 2 (2, 3) times, K1 (2, 1), P2, K6, P2, K1 (2, 1), (P1, K1) 2 (2, 3) times, K1. Rep for sock 2.

Rnd 3 and all odd-numbered rnds

Rows 1 and 2: K1, (P1, K1) 2 (2, 3) times, K1 (2, 1), P2, K6, P2, K1 (2, 1), (K1, P1) 2 (2, 3) times, K1. Rep for sock 2.

Rnd 4

Rows 1 and 2: K1, (K1, P1) 2 (2, 3) times, K1 (2, 1), P2, C6B, P2, K1 (2, 1), (P1, K1) 2 (2, 3) times, K1. Rep for sock 2.

Rnd 6: As rnd 2.

Rnd 7

Place point protectors on tips of resting needle (24") to avoid working with wrong needle, and remove st markers as you get to them. Knit even across both needles and AT SAME TIME move cables to sides as follows:

Row 1: K11 (12, 13), sl next 11 (12, 13) sts onto st holder or waste yarn. Rep for sock 2.

Row 2: Change point protectors to resting needle (16") and carefully sl sts from st holder onto LH side of 24" needle (the one you're getting ready to knit off of). You should have a total of 33 (36, 39) sts on your needle for sock 1. Beg with slipped sts, K22 (24, 26), sl next 11 (12, 13) sts onto st holder. Rep for sock 2 by carefully slipping sts from st holder onto LH side of 24" needle (the one you're getting ready to knit off of). You should have a total of 33 (36, 39) sts on your needle for sock 2. Beg with slipped sts, K22 (24, 26), slip next 11 (12, 13) sts onto st holder. Turn.

Rnd 8

Row 1: Switch point protectors to resting needle (24"). Sl sts from st holder onto LH side of working needle (16")—22 (24, 26) sts for sock 1. Beg with slipped sts, knit even across sock 1. Now sl sts from st holder onto LH side of working needle (16")—22 (24, 26) sts for sock 2. Knit even across to end. Turn.

Both socks have now been turned so that cables no longer sit on front and back but on sides of each sock.

Row 2: Knit even across both socks. Turn.

HEEL FLAP

The heel flap is worked in rows on half of sts (1 needle) only. To help you remember which needle, place point protectors on resting needle before you beg. Remove all st markers.

Unless otherwise specified, sl all sts pw.

Row 1 (RS): Sl 1 wyif, *K1, sl 1 wyib, rep from * to last st, K1.

Row 2 (WS): Sl 1 wyif, purl to last st, K1.

Rep rows 1 and 2 until heel measures 2¼ (2½, 2½)".

TURNING THE HEEL

The heel is turned with the help of short rows, therefore each heel is worked separately, beg with sock 1. Cont to work in rows and with same needle as for heel flap.

Unless otherwise specified, sl all sts pw.

ALL SIZES

Row 1 (RS): Sl 1 wyif, K12 (12, 14), K2tog, K1, turn.

Row 2 (WS): Sl 1 wyif, P5 (3, 5), ssp, P1, turn.

Row 3: Sl 1 kw wyib, K6 (4, 6), K2tog, K1, turn.

Row 4: Sl 1 wyif, P7 (5, 7), ssp, P1, turn.

Row 5: Sl 1 kw wyib, K8 (6, 8), K2 tog, K1, turn.

Row 6: Sl 1 wyif, P9 (7, 9), ssp, P1, turn.

Row 7: Sl 1 kw wyib, K10 (8, 10), K2tog, K1, turn.

SMALL

Row 8: Sl 1 wyif, P11, ssp, *K1*, turn.

Row 9: Sl 1 *pw wyif,* K13, *do not turn*—14 sts rem.

MEDIUM

Row 8: Sl 1 wyif, P9, ssp, P1, turn.

Row 9: Sl 1 kw wyib, K10, K2tog, K1, turn.

Row 10: Sl 1 wyif, P11, ssp, *K1*, turn.

Row 11: Sl 1 *pw wyif,* K13, *do not turn*—14 sts rem.

LARGE

Row 8: Sl 1 wyif, P11, ssp, P1, turn.

Row 9: Sl 1 kw wyib, K12, K2tog, K1, turn.

Row 10: Sl 1 wyif, P13, ssp, *K1*, turn.

Row 11: Sl 1 *pw wyif,* K15, *do not turn*—16 sts rem.

For all sizes, cont with same needle tip, PU 12 (14, 14) sts along side of heel flap, PU 1 gusset st in corner for a total of 13 (15, 15) sts. Move sock to cable and turn heel for sock 2 as for sock 1.

After second heel is turned, cont with same needle tip, PU 12 (14, 14) sts along side of heel flap, PU 1 gusset st in corner for a total of 13 (15, 15) sts. Turn. If necessary, switch point protectors to appropriate needle.

Knit even across instep sts. Turn.

Beg at gusset corner of sock 1, *PU 1 gusset st in corner, PU 12 (14, 14) sts along second side of heel. K7 (7, 8) heel sts, pm, knit across rem heel and gusset sts on other side. Rep from * for sock 2, beg at gusset corner. Turn.

Knit even across all instep sts. Turn.

Both heels are turned and all gusset sts have been picked up. From now on, you'll once again knit in rows as well as rnds. If you still need a little help remembering, cont to switch point protectors to tips of resting needle.

GUSSET DECREASES AND WORKING THE FOOT

Only sole sts are dec.

Rnd 1

Row 1 (sole): Knit across to last 3 sts, K2tog, K1. Rep for sock 2.

Row 2 (instep): Knit even across both socks.

Rnd 2

Row 1 (sole): K1, ssk, knit to end. Rep for sock 2.

Row 2 (instep): Knit even across both socks.

Rep rnds 1 and 2 until 22 (24, 26) sole sts rem per sock, matching number of instep sts for a total of 44 (48, 52) sts per sock.

Remove 1 st marker and leave 1 to mark the needle that starts the rnd. Knit even across sole and instep sts until foot measures approx 6½ (6½, 7)" from back of heel, or until it reaches the base of your big toe when sock is tried on.

SHAPED TOE

Beg dec with sole sts (16" needle).

Rnd 1
Rows 1 (sole) and 2 (instep): K1, ssk, knit to last 3 sts, K2tog, K1. Rep for sock 2.

Rnds 2–4: Knit even across both needles.

Rnd 5
Rows 1 and 2: K1, ssk, knit to last 3 sts, K2tog, K1. Rep for sock 2.

Rnds 6 and 7: Knit even across both needles.

Rnd 8
Rows 1 and 2: K1, ssk, knit to last 3 sts, K2tog, K1. Rep for sock 2, turn.

Rnds 9 and 10: Knit even across both needles.

Rnd 11
Rows 1 and 2: K1, ssk, knit to last 3 sts, K2tog, K1. Rep for sock 2, turn.

Rnd 12: Knit even across both needles.

Rnd 13
Rows 1 and 2: K1, ssk, knit to last 3 sts, K2tog, K1. Rep for sock 2, turn.

Rnd 14: Knit even across both needles.

Rnd 15
Rows 1 and 2: K1, ssk, knit to last 3 sts, K2tog, K1. Rep for sock 2, turn.

Rnd 16: Knit even across both needles.

Rep rnd 15 until 12 (16, 16) total sts rem per sock—6 (8, 8) sts per half.

Cut yarn for both socks, leaving a generous tail (7 to 10").

Use kitchener st to graft toe sts tog for each sock (see page 18).

Cables wander lazily up the leg of Cornucopia in Antique Lace.

Anklets and ruffles

Ruffles come in many textures and are so wonderfully romantic. For mine, I used a variegated mohair/silk blend and I just love them. Feel free to experiment with other yarns though; perhaps you have something in your stash you've been waiting to use! Now is the time—enjoy.

Sizes: Small (Medium, Large)
To fit shoe size: 5-6 (7-9, 10-11)

MATERIALS

MC 2 skeins of Regia Silk from Schachenmayr (55% new wool, 20% silk, 25% polyamide; 50 g/1.75 oz; 200 m/218 yds), color 035 🧵**1**

CC 1 skein of Kid Seta from Madil (70% super kid mohair, 30% silk; 25 g/.88 oz; 210 m/230 yds), color 049 🧵**1**

Size 2 circular needles (16" and 24")

Size 8 circular needles (16" and 24")

Size E or F crochet hook

Point protectors

Stitch markers

Tapestry needle

GAUGE

8½ sts = 1" in St st

SEED STITCH

Rnd 1
Rows 1 and 2: *K1, P1, rep from * across both needles.

Rnd 2
Rows 1 and 2: *P1, K1, rep from * across both needles.

Rep rnds 1 and 2 for patt.

RUFFLE AND CUFF

For all sizes, with CC and larger needles, CO and set up 150 sts for each sock. Purl 1 complete rnd. Avoid using a st marker (it can easily distort the fine mohair blend) by remembering that a new rnd starts with the 16" needle.

Next Rnd
Rows 1 and 2: *P1, P2 tog, rep from * across both needles—100 sts rem per sock.

Work in seed st for 4 rnds, then purl for 4 rnds (8 rnds total).

Change to smaller needles and purl for 3 rnds. Ruffle should measure approx 2".

Change to MC and dec ruffle for your size as follows:

Small: Next Rnd
Rows 1 and 2: P1, P2tog to last 3 sts, P3. Rep for sock 2—52 sts rem per sock.

Medium: Next Rnd

Rows 1 and 2: P3, [(P2tog) 12 times, P2] 3 times, (P2tog) 8 times, P3. Rep for sock 2—56 sts rem per sock.

Large: Next Rnd

Rows 1 and 2: P4, *(P2tog) 10 times, rep from * to last 4 sts, P4. Rep for sock 2—60 sts rem per sock.

LEGS

Work in K1, P1 ribbing until leg measures 4½" from beg of ribbing.

HEEL FLAP

The heel flap is worked in rows on half of the sts (1 needle) only. To help you remember which needle, place point protectors on resting needle before you beg.

Unless otherwise specified, sl all sts pw.

Row 1 (RS): Sl 1 wyif, *K1, sl 1 wyib, rep from * to last st, K1.

Row 2 (WS): Sl 1 wyif, purl to last st, K1.

Rep rows 1 and 2 until heel measures 2¼ (2½, 2½)", ending with a completed purl row.

TURNING THE HEEL

The heel is turned with the help of short rows; therefore, each heel is worked separately, beg with sock 1. Cont to work in rows and with same needle as for heel flap.

Unless otherwise specified, sl all sts pw.

ALL SIZES

Row 1 (RS): Sl 1 wyif, K14 (15, 16), K2tog, K1, turn.

Row 2 (WS): Sl 1 wyif, P5, ssp, P1, turn.

Row 3: Sl 1 *kw wyib*, K6, K2tog, K1, turn.

Row 4: Sl 1 wyif, P7, ssp, P1, turn.

Row 5: Sl 1 *kw wyib*, K8, K2tog, K1, turn.

Row 6: Sl 1 wyif, P9, ssp, P1, turn.

Row 7: Sl 1 *kw wyib*, K10, K2tog, K1, turn.

SMALL

Row 8: Sl 1 wyif, P11, ssp, P1, turn.

Row 9: Sl 1 *kw wyib*, K12, K2tog, K1, turn.

Row 10: Sl 1 wyif, P13, ssp, *K1*, turn.

Row 11: Sl 1 *pw wyif*, K15, *do not turn*—16 sts rem.

MEDIUM

Row 8: Sl 1 wyif, P11, ssp, P1, turn.

Row 9: Sl 1 wyib, K12, K2tog, K1, turn.

Row 10: Sl 1 wyif, P13, ssp, P1, turn.

Row 11: Sl 1 wyib, K14, K2tog, turn.

Row 12: Sl 1 wyif, P14, ssp, turn.

Row 13: Sl 1 *pw wyif*, K15, *do not turn*—16 sts rem.

LARGE

Row 8: Sl 1 wyif, P11, ssp, P1, turn.

Row 9: Sl 1 wyib, K12, K2tog, K1, turn.

Row 10: Sl 1 wyif, P13, ssp, P1, turn.

Row 11: Sl 1 wyib, K14, K2tog, K1, turn.

Row 12: Sl 1 wyif, P15, ssp, *K1*, turn.

Row 13: Sl 1 *pw wyif*, K17, *do not turn*—18 sts rem.

For all sizes, cont with same needle tip, PU 16 (16, 18) sts along side of heel flap, PU 1 gusset st in corner for a total of 17 (17, 19) sts. Move sock to cable and turn heel for sock 2 as for sock 1.

After second heel is turned, cont with same needle tip, PU 16 (16, 18) sts along side of heel flap, PU 1 gusset st in corner for a total of 17 (17, 19) sts. Turn. If necessary, switch point protectors to appropriate needle.

Knit even in St st across all instep sts. Turn.

Beg at gusset corner of sock 1, *PU 1 gusset st in corner, PU 16 (16, 18) sts along second side of heel flap, K8 (8, 9) heel sts, pm, knit across rem heel and gusset sts on other side. Rep from * for sock 2, beg at gusset corner. Turn.

Knit even in St st across all instep sts. Turn.

Both heels are turned and all gusset sts have been picked up. From now on, you'll once again knit in rows as well as rnds. If you still need a little help remembering, cont to switch point protectors to tips of resting needle.

GUSSET DECREASES AND WORKING THE FOOT

Only sole sts are dec.

Rnd 1
Row 1 (sole): Knit across to last 3 sts, K2tog, K1. Rep for sock 2.

Row 2 (instep): Knit even across both socks.

Rnd 2
Row 1 (sole): K1, ssk, knit to end. Rep for sock 2.

Row 2 (instep): Knit even across both socks.

Rep rnds 1 and 2 until 26 (28, 30) sts rem per sock, matching instep sts for a total of 52 (56, 60) sts per sock.

Remove 1 st marker and leave 1 to mark the needle that starts the rnd. Knit even in rnds across sole and instep sts until foot measures approx 7 (7½, 8)" from back of heel, or until it reaches base of big toe when sock is tried on.

SHAPED TOE

Beg dec with sole sts (16" needle).

Rnd 1
Rows 1 (sole) and 2 (instep): K1, ssk, knit to last 3 sts, K2tog, K1. Rep for sock 2.

Rnd 2: Knit even across both needles.

Rep rnds 1 and 2 until 24 total sts rem per sock, 12 sts per half.

Rep rnd 1 until 12 (16, 16) total sts rem per sock, 6 (8, 8) per half.

Cut yarn for both socks, leaving a generous tail (7" to 10").

Use kitchener st to graft toe sts tog for each sock (see page 18).

FINISHING THE RUFFLE

To finish edge of ruffle, work a single crochet into every other st all around edge (see "Single Crochet" on page 17). This will ease ruffle into nice pleats that won't stick out from the sock. Fold cuff over as desired.

Fixation on stripes

If you've never worked with Cascade Yarn's Fixation, it's about time you tried this beautiful elastic, cotton yarn. Not only does it feel wonderful, it also knits up superbly and is an excellent alternative for those who are allergic to wool. Fixation comes in many solid as well as variegated colors, and I think you, too, will love your socks once they are finished.

Sizes: Small (Medium, Large)
To fit shoe size: 5-6 (7-9, 10-11)

MATERIALS

2 (2, 3) skeins of Fixation from Cascade Yarns (98.3% cotton, 1.7% elastic; 50 g/1.75 oz; 186 yds stretched/100 yds relaxed), color 9054 (2)

Size 5 circular needles (16" and 24")

Point protectors

Stitch markers

Tapestry needle

GAUGE

6 sts = 1" in St st

CUFFS

NOTE: To keep correct sequence, begin and end each set as follows:

Small and Large: Beg and end each set with K2 on 16" needle, and with P2 for each set on 24" needle.

Medium: Beg each set on both needles with K2 and end each set with P2.

CO and set up 44 (48, 52) sts. Work in K2, P2 ribbing for 1½" or until desired length.

LEGS

Work in St st until leg measures 6" from CO edge or desired length.

HEEL FLAP

The heel flap is worked in rows on half of the sts (1 needle) only. To help you remember which needle, place point protectors on resting needle before you beg. Remove st marker.

Unless otherwise specified, sl all sts pw.

Row 1 (RS): Sl 1 wyif, *K1, sl 1 wyib, rep from * to last st, K1.

Row 2 (WS): Sl 1 wyif, purl to last st, K1.

Rep rows 1 and 2 until heel measures 2¼ (2½, 2½)".

TURNING THE HEEL

The heel is turned with the help of short rows; therefore, each heel is worked separately, beg with sock 1. Cont to work in rows and with same needle as for heel flap.

Unless otherwise specified, sl all sts pw.

ALL SIZES

Row 1 (RS): Sl 1 wyif, K12, K2tog, K1, turn.

Row 2 (WS): Sl 1 wyif, P5, ssp, P1, turn.

Row 3: Sl 1 *kw wyib*, K6, K2tog, K1, turn.

Row 4: Sl 1 wyif, P7, ssp, P1, turn.

Row 5: Sl 1 kw wyib, K8, K2tog, K1, turn.

Row 6: Sl 1 wyif, P9, ssp, P1, turn.

Row 7: Sl 1 kw wyib, K10, K2tog, K1, turn.

SMALL

Row 8: Sl 1 wyif, P11, ssp, *K1*, turn.

Row 9: Sl 1 *pw wyif*, K13, *do not turn*—14 sts rem.

MEDIUM

Row 8: Sl 1 wyif, P11, ssp, P1, turn.

Row 9: Sl 1 kw wyib, K12, K2tog, K1, turn.

Row 10: Sl 1 wyif, P13, ssp, *K1*, turn.

Row 11: Sl 1 *pw wyif*, K15, *do not turn*—14 sts rem.

LARGE

Row 8: Sl 1 wyif, P11, ssp, P1, turn.

Row 9: Sl 1 kw wyib, K12, K2tog, K1, turn.

Row 10: Sl 1 wyif, P13, ssp, *K1*, turn.

Row 11: Sl 1 *pw wyif*, K15, *do not turn*—16 sts rem.

For all sizes, cont with same needle tip, PU 15 (17, 17) sts along side of heel flap; PU 1 more st in gusset corner for a total of 16 (18, 18) sts. Move sock to cable and turn heel of sock 2 as for sock 1.

After second heel is turned, cont with same needle tip, PU 15 (17, 17) sts along side of heel flap, PU 1 gusset st in corner for a total of 16 (18, 18) sts. Turn. If necessary, switch point protectors to appropriate needle.

Knit even across all instep sts. Turn.

Beg in gusset corner of sock 1, *PU 1 gusset st in corner, PU 15 (17, 17) sts along second side of heel flap, K7 (7, 8) heel sts, pm, knit across rem heel and gusset sts on other side. Rep from * for sock 2, beg at gusset corner. Turn.

Knit even across all instep sts. Turn.

Both heels are turned and all gusset sts have been picked up. From now on, you'll once again knit in rows as well as rnds. If you still need a little help remembering, cont to switch point protectors to tips of resting needle.

GUSSET DECREASES AND WORKING THE FOOT

Only sole sts are dec (16" needle).

Rnd 1

Row 1 (sole): Knit to last 3 sts, K2tog, K1. Rep for sock 2.

Row 2 (instep): Knit even across both socks.

Rnd 2

Row 1 (sole): K1, ssk, knit to end. Rep for sock 2.

Row 2 (instep): Knit even across both socks.

Rep rnds 1 and 2 until 22 (24, 26) sole sts rem per sock, matching number of instep sts for a total of 44 (48, 52) sts per sock.

Remove 1 st marker and leave 1 to mark the needle that starts the rnd. Knit even across sole and instep sts until foot measures approx 6 (6½, 7)" from back of heel, or until it reaches the base of your big toe when sock is tried on.

SHAPED TOE

Beg dec with sole sts (16" needle).

Rnd 1

Needle 1: K1, ssk, knit to last 3 sts, K2tog, K1. Rep for sock 2.

Needle 2: K1, ssk, K10, K2tog, knit to last 3 sts, K2tog, K1. Rep for sock 2.

Rnds 2–4: Knit even across both needles.

Rnd 5/Needles 1 and 2: K1, ssk, knit to last 3 sts, K2tog, K1. Rep for sock 2.

Rnds 6 and 7: Knit even across both needles.

Rnd 8/Needles 1 and 2: K1, ssk, knit to last 3 sts, K2tog, K1. Rep for sock 2.

Rnds 9 and 10: Knit even across both needles.

Rnd 11/Needles 1 and 2: K1, ssk, knit to last 3 sts, K2tog, K1. Rep for sock 2.

Rnd 12: Knit even across both needles.

Rnd 13/Needles 1 and 2: K1, ssk, knit to last 3 sts, K2tog, K1. Rep for sock 2.

Rnd 14: Knit even across both needles.

Rnd 15/Needles 1 and 2: K1, ssk, knit to last 3 sts, K2tog, K1. Rep for sock 2.

Rep rnd 15 until 12 total sts rem per sock, 6 sts per half.

Cut yarn for both socks, leaving a generous tail (7 to 10").

Use kitchener st to graft toe sts tog for each sock (see page 18).

Fixation on lace

While I like all the patterns in this book, this is one of my favorites. I hope you'll not only have fun making these socks (the yarn works up pretty fast) but also love wearing them.

Sizes: Small (Medium, Large)
To fit shoe size: 5-6 (7-9, 10-11)

MATERIALS

2 (2, 3) skeins of Fixation from Cascade Yarns (98.3% cotton, 1.7% elastic; 50 g/1.75 oz; 186 yds stretched/100 yds relaxed), color 5806

Small: Size 4 circular needles (16" for needle 1 and 24" for needle 2)

Medium: Size 5 circular needles (16" for needle 1 and 24" for needle 2)

Large: Size 6 circular needles (16" for needle 1 and 24" for needle 2)

Point protectors

Stitch markers (including 2 lockable)

Tapestry needle

GAUGE

Small: 7 sts = 1" in St st on size 4 needles

Medium: 6 sts = 1" in St st on size 5 needles

Large: 5¾ sts = 1" in St st on size 6 needles

CUFFS/LEGS

To make things less confusing, we're going to name our needles for this pattern. The 16" needle is needle 1 (and will indicate beg of rnd), and the 24" needle is needle 2.

Using needles appropriate for your size, CO 49 sts per sock, but sl 1 st less onto needle 1, leaving 1 extra st on needle 2—24 sts per sock on needle 1, and 25 sts per sock on needle 2. This is necessary to accommodate the uneven number of sts in the lace patt (multiple of 6 sts + 1).

Knit 1 complete rnd.

NOTE: Count stitches after lace pattern rounds regularly. The biggest problem I ran into was forgetting to make my yarn overs.

Work lace patt as follows:

Rnd 1

Needle 1: (K1, K2tog, YO, K1, YO, K2tog tbl) 4 times. Rep for sock 2.

Needle 2: (K1, K2tog, YO, K1, YO, K2tog tbl) 4 times, K1. Rep for sock 2.

Rnd 2 and all even-numbered rnds: Knit across both needles.

Rnd 3

Needle 1: K2tog, (YO, K3, YO, sl 2 sts kw, K1, p2sso) 3 times, YO, K3, YO—1 st remains, sl last st on lockable st marker. Rep for sock 2.

Needle 2: Move st from st marker to RH needle, cont with sts from LH needle and sl 1 st kw, K1, p2sso, (YO, K3, YO, sl 2 sts kw, K1, p2sso) 3 times, YO, K3, YO, K2tog tbl. Rep for sock 2.

Rnd 5

Needle 1: (K1, YO, K2tog tbl, K1, K2tog, YO) 4 times. Rep for sock 2.

Needle 2: (K1, YO, K2tog tbl, K1, K2tog, YO) 4 times, K1. Rep for sock 2.

Rnd 7

Needle 1: K2, (YO, sl 2 sts kw, K1, p2sso, YO, K3) 3 times, YO, sl 2 sts kw, K1, p2sso, YO, K1. Rep for sock 2.

Needle 2: K2, (YO, sl 2 sts kw, K1, p2sso, YO, K3) 3 times, YO, sl 2 sts kw, K1, p2sso, YO, K2. Rep for sock 2.

Rnd 8: Knit across both needles.

Work rnds 1–8 another 5 times. Leg will measure 5½" from CO edge. For a longer/shorter leg, feel free to add or omit one or more complete repetitions. Always end with a finished rnd 8.

HEEL FLAP

The heel flap is worked in rows on half of the sts (1 needle) only. To help you remember which needle, place point protectors on resting needle before you beg.

Unless otherwise specified, sl all sts pw.

Row 1 (RS): Sl 1 wyif, *K1, sl 1 wyib, rep from * to last st, K1.

Row 2 (WS): Sl 1 wyif, purl to last st, K1.

Work rows 1 and 2 another 14 times for a total of 30 rows. Heel measures 2½".

TURNING THE HEEL

The heel is turned with the help of short rows; therefore, each heel is worked separately, beg with sock 1. Cont to work in rows and with same needle as for heel flap.

Unless otherwise specified, sl all sts pw.

Row 1 (RS): Sl 1 wyif, K13, K2tog, K1, turn.

Row 2 (WS): Sl 1 wyif, P5, ssp, P1, turn.

Row 3: Sl 1 kw wyib, K6, K2tog, K1, turn.

Row 4: Sl 1 wyif, P7, ssp, P1, turn.

Row 5: Sl 1 kw wyib, K8, K2tog, K1, turn.

Row 6: Sl 1 wyif, P9, ssp, P1, turn.

Row 7: Sl 1 kw wyib, K10, K2tog, K1, turn.

Row 8: Sl 1 wyif, P11, ssp, P1, turn.

Row 9: Sl 1 kw wyib, K12, K2tog, turn.

Row 10: Sl 1 wyif, P12, ssp, turn.

Row 11: Sl 1 *pw wyif*, K13, *do not turn*—14 sts rem.

Cont with the same needle tip, PU 15 sts along side of heel flap, PU 1 gusset st in corner for a total of 16 sts. Move sock to cable and turn heel of sock 2 as for sock 1.

After second heel is turned, cont with same needle tip, PU 15 sts along side of heel flap, PU 1 gusset st in corner for a total of 16 sts. Turn. If necessary, switch point protectors to appropriate needle.

*Knit across 25 instep sts as follows: (K1, K2tog, YO, K1, YO, K2tog tbl) 4 times, K1. Rep from * for sock 2, turn.

Beg at gusset corner of sock 1, **PU 1 gusset st in corner, PU 15 sts along second side of heel flap, K7 heel sts, pm, knit across rem heel and gusset sts on other side. Rep from ** for sock 2, beg at gusset corner. Turn.

Knit even in St st across all instep sts. Turn.

Both heels are turned and all gusset sts have been picked up. From now on, you'll once again knit in rows as well as rnds. If you still need a little help remembering, cont to switch point protectors to tips of resting needle.

GUSSET DECREASES AND WORKING THE FOOT

Only sole sts are dec (16" needle).

Rnd 1

Needle 1 (sole): Knit to last 3 sts, K2tog, K1. Rep for sock 2.

Needle 2 (instep): Skp, (YO, K3, YO, sl 2 sts kw, K1, p2sso) 3 times, YO, K3, YO, K2tog tbl. Rep for sock 2.

Rnd 2

Needle 1 (sole): K1, ssk, knit to end. Rep for sock 2.

Needle 2 (instep): Knit across both socks.

Rnd 3

Needle 1 (sole): Knit to last 3 sts, K2tog, K1. Rep for sock 2.

Needle 2 (instep): (K1, YO, K2tog tbl, K1, K2tog, YO) 4 times, K1. Rep for sock 2.

Rnd 4

Needle 1 (sole): K1, ssk, knit to end. Rep for sock 2.

Needle 2 (instep): Knit across both socks.

Rnd 5

Needle 1 (sole): Knit to last 3 sts, K2tog, K1. Rep for sock 2.

Needle 2 (instep): K2, (YO, sl 2 sts kw, K1, p2sso, YO, K3) 3 times, YO, sl 2 sts kw, K1, p2sso, YO, K2. Rep for sock 2.

Rnd 6

Needle 1 (sole): K1, ssk, knit to end. Rep for sock 2.

Needle 2 (instep): Knit across both socks.

Rnd 7

Needle 1 (sole): Knit to last 3 sts, K2tog, K1. Rep for sock 2.

Needle 2 (instep): (K1, K2tog, YO, K1, YO, K2tog tbl) 4 times, K1. Rep for sock 2.

Rnd 8

Needle 1 (sole): K1, ssk, knit to end. Rep for sock 2.

Needle 2 (instep): Knit across both socks.

Rep rnds 1–8 once more, then rnds 1–6 once—24 sole sts rem per sock, total 49 sts per sock.

Remove 1 st marker and leave 1 to mark the needle that starts the rnd. Work rnds 1–8 as follows until foot measures approx 6½ (7, 7½)" from back of heel, or until it reaches the base of your big toe when sock is tried on.

Rnd 1

Needle 1: Knit in St st across both socks.

Needle 2: (K1, K2tog, YO, K1, YO, K2tog tbl) 4 times, K1. Rep for sock 2.

Rnd 2 and all even-numbered rnds: Knit in St st across both needles.

Rnd 3

Needle 1: Knit in St st across both socks.

Needle 2: Sl 1 st kw, K1, psso, (YO, K3, YO, sl 2 sts kw, K1, p2sso) 3 times, YO, K3, YO, K2tog tbl. Rep for sock 2.

Rnd 5

Needle 1: Knit in St st across both socks.

Needle 2: (K1, YO, K2tog tbl, K1, K2tog, YO) 4 times, K1. Rep for sock 2.

Rnd 7

Needle 1: Knit in St st across both socks.

Needle 2: K2, (YO, sl 2 sts kw, K1, p2sso, YO, K3) 3 times, YO, sl 2 sts kw, K1, p2sso, YO, K2. Rep for sock 2.

Rnd 8: Knit in St st across both needles.

SHAPED TOE

Beg dec with sole sts (16" needle).

The extra K2tog in rnd 1 (needle 2) brings sole and instep to same st count, which is needed for kitchener st later on.

Rnd 1

Needle 1: K1, ssk, knit to last 3 sts, K2tog, K1. Rep for sock 2.

Needle 2: K1, ssk, K10, K2tog, knit to last 3 sts, K2tog, K1. Rep for sock 2.

Rnds 2–4: Knit even across both needles.

Rnd 5

Needles 1 and 2: K1, ssk, knit to last 3 sts, K2tog, K1. Rep for sock 2.

Rnds 6 and 7: Knit even across both needles.

Rnd 8

Needles 1 and 2: K1, ssk, knit to last 3 sts, K2tog, K1. Rep for sock 2.

Rnds 9 and 10: Knit even across both needles.

Rnd 11

Needles 1 and 2: K1, ssk, knit to last 3 sts, K2tog, K1. Rep for sock 2.

Rnd 12: Knit even across both needles.

Rnd 13

Needles 1 and 2: K1, ssk, knit to last 3 sts, K2tog, K1. Rep for sock 2.

Rnd 14: Knit even across both needles.

Rnd 15

Needles 1 and 2: K1, ssk, knit to last 3 sts, K2tog, K1. Rep for sock 2.

Rep rnd 15 until 12 total sts rem per sock, 6 sts per half.

Cut yarn for both socks, leaving a generous tail (7 to 10").

Use kitchener st to graft toe sts tog for each sock (see page 18).

Fixation offers endless colors, but how can you resist Pink Lemonade 3077?

Diamonds and lace

This beautiful diamond lace pattern has a rolled cuff and ribbed ankle, which makes it an excellent choice for working with less-elastic yarns, such as cotton and linen blends, because the ribbed ankle supports the sock leg comfortably. Its biggest challenge is the occasional yarn over at the beginning and end of a row. Make sure you count your stitches regularly to avoid losing any and having to unknit rows.

Sizes: Small (Medium, Large)
To fit shoe size: 5-6 (7-9, 10-11)

MATERIALS

2 skeins of Regia Color 4-ply from Schachenmayr (75% new wool, 25% polyamide; 50 g/1.75 oz; 210 m/230 yds), color 1912 (**1**)

Small: Size 1 circular needles (16" and 24")

Medium: Size 2 circular needles (16" and 24")

Large: Size 3 circular needles (16" and 24")

Point protectors

Stitch markers (optional: 1 lockable)

Tapestry needle

GAUGE

Small: 8 sts = 1" in St st on size 1 needles

Medium: 7½ sts = 1" in St st on size 2 needles

Large: 6¾ sts = 1" in St st on size 3 needles

CUFFS

To make things less confusing, we're going to name our needles for this pattern. The 16" needle is needle 1, and the 24" needle is needle 2.

CO and set up 60 sts for each sock. You should be ready to work needle 1 (16") first.

Knit 8 rnds (½") even in St st.

TIP: Needle 1 will mark the beginning of the round from now on because a stitch marker will hinder smooth knitting of the lace pattern. If you don't feel confident enough to do this without a reminder, attach a lockable stitch marker to the cast-on edge of the first sock to be worked.

LEGS

Working a YO at the end of a set of sts: This pattern requires you to frequently create a YO at the end (and beg) of each set of 30 sts on needles 1 and 2. To create the *end YO,* work 3 repetitions of lace patt for first sock (30 sts), ending with K2tog. Let your working yarn hang *in front of needle 2 and toward you.* Now rep lace patt for sock 2 on same needle and then turn your work. Before beg patt row of needle 2, run working yarn of sock 1 *under, then behind and over needle 1,* in front of last worked st, thus creating a YO at end of sock 2 for previous row. Work first sock in patt. After you've finished last K2tog, remember to let your working yarn hang in front of needle 1 and toward you. Notice how working yarn for sock 2 simply hangs behind needle 1. Take this strand and pull it *under, then behind and over needle 1 toward you,* once again creating a YO for previous row 1. Now knit first st of sock 2 in current row and remember to squeeze needle and cable close together to avoid a larger hole than necessary. Turn.

You've just knitted a complete rnd; however, you still have to create the YOs for the sts sitting on needle 2. Beg next rnd by running working yarn *under, then behind and over needle 2* in front of last worked st, thus creating a YO at end of sock 2 in previous row. After you've finished sock 1 of this row, let your working yarn hang *over and behind needle 2* as described in "The Basic Sock Pattern" on page 20 to avoid creating unwanted sts (you don't need another YO right now). As you come to second sock, take working yarn and once again pull

it *under, then behind and over needle 1 toward you* to create needed end YO for previous row.

The lace patt is charted on page 74 as well as written out on page 71 for those of you who feel uncomfortable following a chart. I highly recommend that you at least try to use the chart. It leaves less room for error and is easier to understand after you've familiarized yourself with the symbols and have knitted the first few rows.

NOTE: The written patt lists rnds only, and each rnd consists of 2 rows (needle 1 and needle 2).

For example, the instruction given for rnd 1 is as follows:

Rnd 1: (K8, K2tog, YO) 3 times. Rep for sock 2.

This means that you work the rows as follows:

Row 1/Needle 1: (K8, K2tog, YO) 3 times. Rep for sock 2.

Row 2/Needle 2: (K8, K2tog, YO) 3 times. Rep for sock 2.

So for every rnd, you'll work the same instructions on needle 1 and needle 2.

Work lace patt as follows:

Rnd 1: (K8, K2tog, YO) 3 times. Rep for sock 2.

Rnd 2 and all even-numbered rnds: Knit across both needles. Make sure YOs are in place where indicated. After you've finished even-numbered rnds, count sts to verify correct amount on your needles.

Rnd 3: (YO, [hold needles ready to start, scoop up working yarn back to front with RH needle, then beg knitting off LH needle], ssk, K5, K2tog, YO, K1) 3 times. Rep for sock 2.

Rnd 5: (K1, YO, ssk, K3, K2tog, YO, K2tog, YO) 3 times. Rep for sock 2.

Rnd 7: (YO, ssk, YO, ssk, K1, K2tog, YO, K2tog, YO, K1) 3 times. Rep for sock 2.

Rnd 9: (K1, YO, ssk, YO, sk2p, YO, K2tog, YO, K2) 3 times. Rep for sock 2.

Rnd 11: (K2, YO, ssk, YO, sk2p, YO, K3) 3 times. Rep for sock 2.

Rnd 13: (K3, YO, sk2p, YO, K4) 3 times. Rep for sock 2.

Rnd 15: (K8, K2tog, YO) 3 times. Rep for sock 2.

Rnd 17: (YO, ssk, K5, K2tog, YO, K1) 3 times. Rep for sock 2.

Rnd 19: (K1, YO, ssk, K3, K2tog, YO, K2tog, YO) 3 times. Rep for sock 2.

Rnd 21: (YO, ssk, YO, ssk, K1, K2tog, YO, K2tog, YO, K1) 3 times. Rep for sock 2.

Rnd 23: (K1, YO, ssk, YO, sl 2 kw, K1, p2sso, YO, K2tog, YO, K2tog, YO) 3 times. Rep for sock 2.

Rnd 25: (YO, ssk, YO, ssk, K1, K2tog, YO, K2tog, YO, K1) 3 times. Rep for sock 2.

Rnd 27: (K1, YO, ssk, K3, K2tog, YO, K2tog, YO) 3 times. Rep for sock 2.

Rnd 29: (YO, ssk, K5, K2tog, YO, K1) 3 times. Rep for sock 2.

Rnd 31: (K8, K2tog, YO) 3 times. Rep for sock 2.

Rnd 33: (K3, YO, sk2p, YO, K4) 3 times. Rep for sock 2.

Rnd 35: (K2, YO, K2tog, YO, sk2p, YO, K3) 3 times. Rep for sock 2.

Rnd 37: (K1, YO, K2tog, YO, sk2p, YO, ssk, YO, K2) 3 times. Rep for sock 2.

Rnd 39: (YO, K2tog, YO, K2tog, K1, ssk, YO, ssk, YO, K1) 3 times. Rep for sock 2.

Rnd 41: (K1, YO, K2tog, K3, ssk, YO, ssk, YO) 3 times. Rep for sock 2.

Rnd 43: (YO, K2tog, K5, ssk, YO, K1) 3 times. Rep for sock 2.

Rnd 45: (K8, ssk, YO) 3 times. Rep for sock 2.

Rnd 46: Knit across both needles.

ANKLE RIBBING

The rolled edge as well as the lace patt will leave your sock leg a little looser than normal. To keep your sock from slipping, you'll need to work a couple of dec and an ankle ribbing for a snugger fit.

Rnd 1

Needles 1 and 2: (K1, P1) 5 times, K2tog, P1, (K1, P1) twice, K2tog, P1, (K1, P1) 5 times. Rep for sock 2—56 total sts per sock rem.

Work in K1, P1 ribbing as established without further dec for 11 more rnds (1¼").

Knit 1 rnd across both needles.

HEEL FLAP

The heel flap is worked in rows on half of the sts (1 needle) only. To help you remember which needle, place point protectors on resting needle before you beg.

Unless otherwise specified, sl all sts pw.

Row 1 (RS): Sl 1 wyif, *K1, sl 1 wyib, rep from * to last st, K1.

Row 2 (WS): Sl 1 wyif, purl to last st, K1.

Work rows 1 and 2 another 12 times for a total of 26 rows. Heel flap measures 2½".

TURNING THE HEEL

Remember, the heel is turned with the help of short rows; therefore, each heel is worked separately, beg with sock 1. Cont to work in rows and with same needle as for heel flap.

Unless otherwise specified, sl all sts pw.

Row 1 (RS): Sl 1 wyif, K15, K2tog, K1, turn.

Row 2 (WS): Sl 1 wyif, P5, ssp, P1, turn.

Row 3: Sl 1 *kw wyib*, K6, K2tog, K1, turn.

Row 4: Sl 1 wyif, P7, ssp, P1, turn.

Row 5: Sl 1 kw wyib, K8, K2tog, K1, turn.

Row 6: Sl 1 wyif, P9, ssp, P1, turn.

Row 7: Sl 1 kw wyib, K10, K2tog, K1, turn.

Row 8: Sl 1 wyif, P11, ssp, P1, turn.

Row 9: Sl 1 kw wyib, K12, K2tog, K1, turn.

Row 10: Sl 1 wyif, P13, ssp, P1, turn.

Row 11: Sl 1 kw wyib, K14, K2tog, turn.

Row 12: Sl 1 wyif, P14, ssp, turn.

Row 13: Sl 1 *wyif*, K15, *do not turn work*—16 sts rem.

Cont with the same needle tip, PU 14 sts along side of heel flap, PU 1 st in gusset corner for a total of 15 sts. Move sock to cable and turn heel of sock 2 as for sock 1.

After second heel is turned, cont with same needle tip, PU 14 sts along side of heel flap, PU 1 gusset st in corner for a total of 15 sts. Turn. If necessary, switch point protectors appropriately.

Knit even across all instep sts. Turn.

Beg at gusset corner of sock 1, *PU 1 gusset st in corner, PU 14 sts along second side of heel flap, K8 heel sts, pm, knit across rem heel and gusset sts on other side. Rep from * for sock 2, beg at gusset corner. Turn.

Knit even across all instep sts.

Both heels are turned and all gusset sts have been picked up. From now on, you'll once again knit in rows as well as rnds. If you still need a little help remembering, cont to switch point protectors to tips of resting needle.

GUSSET DECREASES AND WORKING THE FOOT

Only sole sts are dec (needle 1).

Rnd 1
Row 1 (sole): Knit to last 3 sts, K2tog, K1. Rep for sock 2.

Row 2 (instep): Knit even across both socks.

Rnd 2
Row 1 (sole): K1, ssk, knit to end. Rep for sock 2.

Row 2 (instep): Knit even across both socks.

Rep rnds 1 and 2 until 28 sole sts rem per sock, matching number of instep sts for a total of 56 sts per sock.

Remove 1 st marker and leave 1 to mark the needle that starts the rnd. Knit even across sole and instep sts until foot measures approx 7 (7½, 8)" from back of heel, or until it reaches the base of your big toe when sock is tried on.

SHAPED TOE

Beg dec with sole sts (needle 1).

Rnd 1
Rows 1 (sole) and 2 (instep): K1, ssk, knit to last 3 sts, K2tog, K1. Rep for sock 2.

Rnd 2: Knit even across both needles.

Rep rnds 1 and 2 until 28 total sts rem per sock, 14 sts per half.

Rep rnd 1 until 20 total sts rem per sock, 10 sts per half.

Cut yarn for both socks, leaving a generous tail (7 to 10").

Use kitchener st to graft toe sts tog for each sock (see page 18).

Even black diamonds steal the show. Here the pattern is shown in Regia Color 4-ply in color 5097.

Diamonds and Lace Pattern Chart

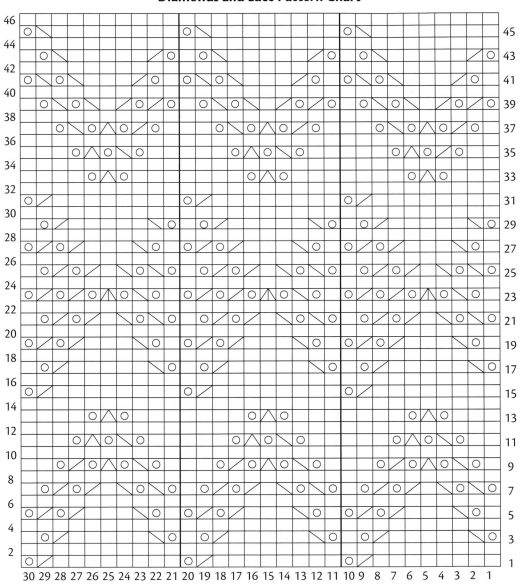

Chart Symbol Key

	Knit		K2tog
	YO		sk2p
	SSK		sl 2 kw, K1, p2sso

Converting Patterns from Double-Pointed to Circular Needles

Once you've become comfortable with the basic pattern, you'll be able to convert any sock pattern from double-pointed needles to two circular needles. Conventional sock patterns use either three or four double-pointed needles to set up the sock. For clarification, the needles are numbered and carry specific stitches—for example, the instep or part of the heel. Whatever the case may be, when using two circular needles, the stitches are simply divided in half with one needle carrying all the instep stitches and the other carrying all the heel or sole stitches.

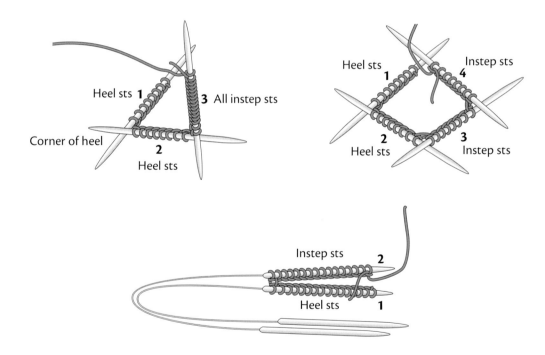

In traditional sock patterns, knitters have to work with multiple needles, remember which needle corresponds to which number of stitches, and can only work on one sock at a time. The cuff and leg are worked in the round for so many inches. Then the real fun begins. For the heel flap and turning of the heel, knitters have to remember which number of stitches belongs to which needle, and switch stitches from one needle to another ("M1, sl 1, dec 1") until finally all heel stitches are sitting on one needle. But it doesn't stop there; once finished with the heel, stitches have to get moved and shifted again to accommodate the gusset, which is worked on two needles (but which ones?).

Using circular needles is sock knitting utterly simplified. Take a look at the traditional pattern you've picked to convert.

1. Cast on and set up X amount of sts on your two circular needles.

2. Work cuff and leg in the round to desired length.

3. Work heel flap (sitting on one circular needle) back and forth, using traditional pattern to desired length.

4. Ignore all shifting of stitches in the traditional pattern and go straight to heel-turning instructions. Since the heel is turned on one needle, regardless of how many double-pointed needles are indicated, turn your heel exactly as described in the pattern, using the circular needle that holds the heel flap.

5. Once the heel is turned, ignore all shifting of stitches in the traditional pattern and simply find the amount of stitches to be picked up for the gusset. Then follow the circular needle instructions and pick up all gusset stitches plus the extra corner stitches.

6. From now on, you can ignore the traditional pattern altogether and follow the circular pattern to decrease the gusset stitches back to the original stitch count. Then work the foot.

7. For the toe, you can choose one of the decreases in this book, decrease every other round or use the gradual decrease for a more rounded effect, or you can use the decrease in the traditional pattern. Remember that all decreases always take place in one round and at both sides of both circular needles.

8. Check the traditional pattern to see how many toe stitches are left before it's closed with the kitchener stitch and decrease accordingly.

Once you've converted a few patterns, you'll get used to quickly gathering all the necessary information needed from the traditional pattern and transferring it to your circular needles.

Abbreviations and Glossary

approx	approximately	PU	pick up and knit
beg	begin(ning)	pw	purlwise
BO	bind off	rem	remain(ing)
CC	contrasting color	rep(s)	repeat(s)
cn	cable needle	RH	right hand
CO	cast on	rnd(s)	round(s)
cont	continue(ing)	RS	right side
dec	decrease(s)(ing)	skp	slip 1, knit 1, pass slipped stitch over knit stitch (see page 15)
EOR	every other row		
g	gram(s)	sk2p	slip 1, K2tog, pass slipped stitch over the K2tog (see page 16)
inc	increase(s)(ing)		
K	knit	sl	slip
K2tog	knit 2 stitches together (see page 14)	sl 2, K1, p2sso	slip 2 knitwise, K1, pass 2 slipped stitches over knit stitch (see page 16)
kw	knitwise		
LH	left hand	sl st	slip stitch
M1	make 1 stitch (see page 17)	ssk	slip, slip, knit (see page 14)
MC	main color	ssp	slip, slip, purl (see page 15)
oz	ounces	st(s)	stitch(es)
P	purl	St st	stockinette stitch
patt	pattern	tbl	through back loop
pm	place marker	wyib	with yarn in back
p2sso	pass 2 slipped stitches over together	wyif	with yarn in front
P2tog	purl 2 stitches together (see page 14)	WS	wrong side
P3tog	purl 3 stitches together	yds	yards
psso	pass slipped stitch over	YO	yarn over

Useful Information

YARN-WEIGHT SYMBOLS						
Yarn Weight Symbol and Category Names	**1** Super Fine	**2** Fine	**3** Light	**4** Medium	**5** Bulky	**6** Super Bulky
Type of Yarns in Category	Sock, Fingering, Baby	Sport, Baby	DK, Light Worsted	Worsted, Afghan, Aran	Chunky, Craft, Rug	Bulky, Roving
Knit Gauge Ranges in Stockinette Stitch to 4"	27 to 32 sts	23 to 26 sts	21 to 24 sts	16 to 20 sts	12 to 15 sts	6 to 11 sts
Recommended Needle in U.S. Size Range	1 to 3	3 to 5	5 to 7	7 to 9	9 to 11	11 and larger
Recommended Needle in Metric Size Range	2.25 to 3.25 mm	3.25 to 3.75 mm	3.75 to 4.5 mm	4.5 to 5.5 mm	5.5 to 8 mm	8 mm and larger

SKILL LEVELS

■□□□ **Beginner:** Projects for first-time knitters using basic knit and purl stitches. Minimal shaping.

■■□□ **Easy:** Project using basic stitches, repetitive stitch patterns, and simple color changes. Simple shaping and finishing.

■■■□ **Intermediate:** Projects using a variety of stitches, such as basic cables and lace; simple intarsia; and techniques for double-pointed needles and knitting in the round. Midlevel shaping.

■■■■ **Experienced:** Projects using advanced techniques and stitches, such as short rows, Fair Isle, more intricate intarsia, cables, lace patterns, and numerous color changes.

METRIC CONVERSIONS

Yards x .91 = meters

Meters x 1.09 = yards

Grams x .0352 = ounces

Ounces x 28.35 = grams

YARN-CARE SYMBOLS

Washing

- Do not wash
- Hand wash in warm water
- Hand wash at stated temperature
- Machine wash

- Do not tumble dry
- Tumble drying OK
- Dry flat
- No bleach
- Chlorine bleach OK

Pressing

- Do not iron
- Cool iron
- Warm iron
- Hot iron

Yarn Sources

Contact the following companies to locate shops that carry the yarns featured in this book.

Araucania Yarns
www.araucaniayarns.com
www.knittingfever.com
Patagonia Nature Cotton

Cascade Yarns
www.cascadeyarns.com
Cascade 220 Tweed
Fixation
Kid Seta

Kolláge Yarns
www.kollageyarns.com
Cornucopia

Schaefer Yarn Company, Ltd.
www.schaeferyarn.com
Anne

Westminster Fibers, Inc.
Schachenmayr Yarn
www.westminsterfibers.com
Regia Color 4-ply
Regia Silk

Knitting and Crochet Titles

Martingale® & COMPANY

America's Best-Loved Craft & Hobby Books®
America's Best-Loved Knitting Books®

CROCHET

Creative Crochet

Crochet for Babies
and Toddlers

Crochet for Tots

Crochet from the Heart

Crocheted Pursenalities—*New!*

Crocheted Socks!

Cute Crochet for Kids

The Essential Book of
Crochet Techniques

Eye-Catching Crochet

First Crochet

Fun and Funky Crochet

Funky Chunky
Crocheted Accessories

**The Little Box of Crochet
for Baby—*New!***

The Little Box of
Crocheted Bags

The Little Box of Crocheted Hats
and Scarves

The Little Box of Crocheted
Ponchos and Wraps

**The Little Box of Crocheted
Scarves—*New!***

More Crocheted
Aran Sweaters

KNITTING

200 Knitted Blocks

365 Knitting Stitches a Year:
Perpetual Calendar

A to Z of Knitting—*New!*

Big Knitting

Blankets, Hats, and Booties

Double Exposure

Everyday Style

Fair Isle Sweaters Simplified

First Knits

Fun and Funky Knitting

Funky Chunky
Knitted Accessories

Handknit Style

Handknit Style II

Knits, Knots, Buttons,
and Bows

Knitted Shawls, Stoles,
and Scarves

The Knitter's Book of
Finishing Techniques

**Knitting Beyond the Basics—
*New!***

Knitting with Gigi—*New!*

Lavish Lace

The Little Box of Knits
for Baby

The Little Box of Knitted
Ponchos and Wraps

The Little Box of
Knitted Throws

The Little Box of Scarves

The Little Box of Scarves II

Modern Classics

More Sensational Knitted Socks—*New!*

The Pleasures of Knitting

Pursenalities

Pursenality Plus

Ribbon Style

Romantic Style

Sarah Dallas Knitting

Saturday Sweaters

Sensational Knitted Socks

Silk Knits

Simply Beautiful Sweaters

**Special Little Knits from
Just One Skein—*New!***

Top Down Sweaters—*New!*

The Ultimate Knitted Tee

Wrapped in Comfort—*New!*

The Yarn Stash Workbook

Our books are available at bookstores and your favorite craft, fabric, and yarn retailers.
If you don't see the title you're looking for, visit us at **www.martingale-pub.com** or contact us at:

1-800-426-3126

International: 1-425-483-3313 • Fax: 1-425-486-7596 • Email: info@martingale-pub.com

3/07 Knit